SCHOLASTIC Spelling™

Louisa Moats and Barbara Foorman

Welcome!

Contents

3

Contents

Contents

Spelling Strategies
Word Study Path

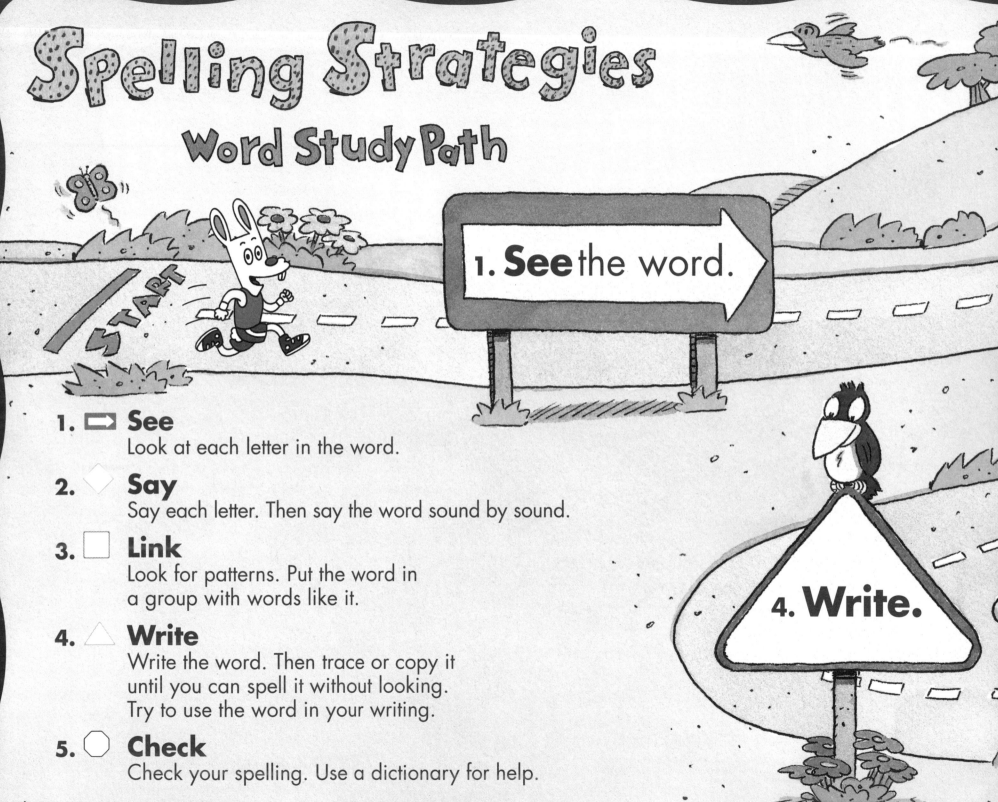

1. See the word.

4. Write.

1. ▭ **See**
   Look at each letter in the word.

2. ◇ **Say**
   Say each letter. Then say the word sound by sound.

3. □ **Link**
   Look for patterns. Put the word in a group with words like it.

4. △ **Write**
   Write the word. Then trace or copy it until you can spell it without looking. Try to use the word in your writing.

5. ◯ **Check**
   Check your spelling. Use a dictionary for help.

2. **Say** it slowly.

3. **Link** sounds and letters.

5. **Check.**

The Letters m s l a   Mm   Ss

Just Like Me

I sat on the sand.
Just like me.
I looked in the mirror.
Just like me.
I saw my mom.
She saw me.

Objectives: Children listen to the choral poem; circle each picture whose name begins with the same sound as *man;* and put an X on each picture whose name begins with the same sound as *sun.* Children listen again for words that begin with /m/ and /s/.

At-Home Activity: With your child, look at home for things whose names begin with the same sound as *man* and as *sun.*

Name . . . .

Mm Ss

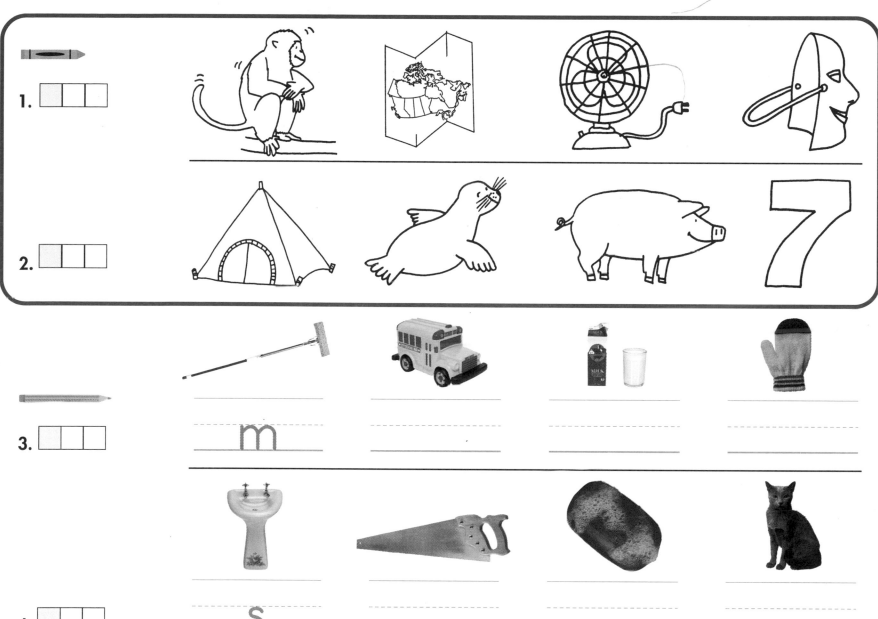

1.

2.

3.   m

4.   s

Objectives: With children, name each picture. Children colour pictures whose names begin with /m/ for row 1 and /s/ for row 2. For row 3, they write *m* below each picture whose name begins with /m/. Repeat for row 4 with *s*.

At-Home Activity: With your child, look through a magazine. Take turns pointing to pictures of things whose names begin with the same sound as *mat*. Then repeat with pictures of things whose names begin with the same sound as *soap*.

Ll  Aa

I Like Apples

Way up high in the apple tree,

Two little apples smiled at me.

I shook the tree as long as I could.

And down came the apples,

Mmm, they look good!

Objectives: Children listen to the action rhyme; circle each picture whose name begins with the same sound as *lamp;* and put an X on each picture whose name has /a/ as in *apple* and *hat.* Children listen to the action rhyme again for words that begin with /l/ and /a/.

At-Home Activity: With your child, cut out pictures of objects from old magazines whose names begin with the same sound as *lamp* or whose names have the sound of *a* as in *apple* and *cat.*

Name

Ll **Aa**

1.

2.

3.

4.

a

Objectives: With children, name each picture. Children colour pictures whose names begin with /l/ for row 1 and contain /a/ as in *apple* and *cat* for row 2. For row 3, they write *l* below each picture whose name begins with /l/. Repeat for row 4 for picture names that contain /a/.

At-Home Activity: With your child, make up silly sentences, using words that begin with the same sound as *lamp* or that contain the sound of *a* as in *apple* and *cat*. For example, *Lucky Lenny laughed at the lazy lion. Abby sat and canned apples.*

The Letters t p i f   Tt  Pp

How Many?

A pig, pony, tiger, and
polar bear,
Saw a panda and
turkey at a fair.
Along came a puppy
and a penguin down
the road,
As well as a turtle,
carrying its load.
Under a tiny umbrella
they all met.
How many animal
friends got wet?

None. It wasn't raining!

Objectives: Children listen to the riddle; circle each picture whose name begins with the same sound as *top;* and put an X on each picture whose name begins with the same sound as *pig.* Children listen again for words that begin with /t/ and /p/.

At-Home Activity: With your child, gather objects whose names begin with the same sound as *table* and place them on a table. Then gather objects whose names begin with the same sound as *pot* and place them in a big pot.

Name .....

Tt   Pp

1.

2.

3.   t

4.   p

Objectives: With children, name each picture. Children colour pictures whose names begin with /t/ for row 1 and /p/ for row 2. For row 3, they write *t* below each picture whose name begins with /t/. Repeat for row 4 with *p*.

At-Home Activity: Take turns doing things that begin with the same sound as *top*. For example, talk or touch your toes. Then take turns naming foods whose names begin with the same sound as *pig*. For example, *popcorn* and *peanuts*.

Ii  Ff

Four Seasons

Spring is itchy, twitchy;
breezy, wheezy.
Summer is sunny, funny;
fishy, squishy.
Fall is foggy, smoggy;
chilly, willy.
Winter is slippy, nippy;
fuzzy-wuzzy.

Objectives: Children listen to the poem; circle each picture whose name has /i/ as in *insect* and *pig*; underline each picture whose name begins with the same sound as *fish*. Children listen again for words that have /i/ and /f/. Point out that *fishy* has both /i/ and /f/.

At-Home Activity: With your child, find things around the house whose names have the sound of *i* as in *insect* and *pig*. Find things whose names begin with the same sound as *fish*.

Name ....

Ii  Ff

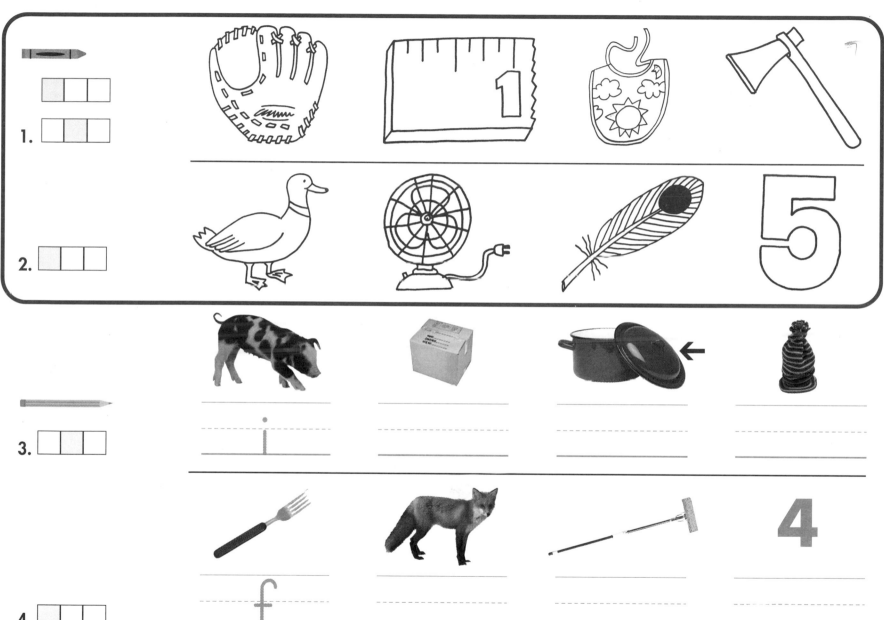

1.

2.

3.

i

4.

f

Objectives: With children, name each picture. Children colour pictures whose names contain /ɪ/ as in *insect* and *pig* for row 1 and /f/ for row 2. For row 3, they write *i* below each picture whose name contains /ɪ/. Repeat for row 4 with *f*.

At-Home Activity: With your child, make up silly rhyming word pairs with the sound of *i* as in *insect* and *pig*. For example, *itsy-bitsy, itchy-nitchy, icky-sticky*. Then take turns drawing pictures of things whose names begin with the same sound as *fish*.

What Kind of Noise?

What kind of noise annoys a dandy duck?

A noisy noise annoys a dandy duck!

Objectives: Children listen to the tongue twister; circle each picture whose name begins with the same sound as *nest;* and put an X on each picture whose name begins with the same sound as *dog.* Children listen to the tongue twister again for words that begin with /n/ and /d/.

At-Home Activity: With your child, tap a nickel on things in your home whose names begin with the same sound as *nickel.* Then tap a dime on things whose names begin with the same sound as *dime.*

Nn  Dd

1.

2.

3.

n

4.

d

Objectives: Together with children, name each picture. Children colour pictures whose names begin with /n/ for row 1 and /d/ for row 2. For row 3, they write *n* below each picture whose name begins with /n/. Repeat for row 4 with *d*.

At-Home Activity: Dance with your child as you take turns saying words that begin with the same sound as *dance*. Then rest by pretending to take a nap and whispering words that begin with the same sound as *nap*.

Oo

Animals

Can you hop like a rabbit?

Can you jump like a frog?

Can you walk like an ox?

Can you run like a dog?

Can you fly like a bird?

Can you swim like an otter?

And be still like a child—

As still as this?

Objectives: Children listen to the action rhyme, then circle each picture whose name has /o/ as in *octopus* and *mop*. They listen to the action rhyme again for words that contain /o/.

At-Home Activity: Together with your child, think about toys and games that have the sound of *o* as in *octopus* and *mop*. For example, Jack-in-the-*Box*, *hopscotch*, "*Pop* Goes the Weasel."

Readiness

Name

Oo

1.

2.

3.

O

4.    **10**

O

Objectives: With children, name each picture. Children colour pictures whose names begin with /o/ for row 1 and whose names have /o/ in the middle for row 2. They write o below each picture whose name begins with /o/ for row 3 and has medial /o/ for row 4.

At-Home Activity: With your child, name friends and family members whose names have the sound of o as in *Ozzie* and *Tom*.

The Letters *n d o* 19

Readiness · Name.................................

The Letters h c w b Hh  Cc

Cows

This little cow eats grass,

This little cow eats hay,

This little cow looks over
the hedge,

This little cow runs away.

And this big cow does
nothing at all

But lie in the fields all day.

Objectives: Children listen to the fingerplay, then circle each picture whose name begins with the same sound as *hat*. They underline each picture whose name begins with the same sound as *cat*. Children listen to the fingerplay again for words that begin with /h/ and /k/.

At-Home Activity: As you travel with your child, look for things whose names begin with the same sound as *hay* and as *cow*.

Name

Hh **Cc**

1.

2.

3.   h

4.   c

Objectives: With children, name each picture. Children colour pictures whose names begin with /h/ for row 1 and /k/ for row 2. For row 3, they write *h* below each picture whose name begins with /h/. Repeat for row 4 with *c*.

At-Home Activity: With your child, hop on one foot as you take turns naming words that begin with the same sound as *hop*. Invite your child to identify things whose names begin with the same sound as *car* that he or she might see while riding in a car.

Ww Bb

Wakey, Wakey

Wakey, wakey, rise
and shine,
Make your bed,
And then make mine.

Objectives: Children listen to the poem; circle each picture whose name begins with the same sound as *wig;* and put an X on each picture whose name begins with the same sound as *ball.* Children listen to the poem again for words that begin with /w/ and /b/.

At-Home Activity: With your child, find things at home whose names begin with the same sound as *wig,* and label them with self-sticking notes. Together, gather things whose names begin with the same sound as *bag,* and put them in a bag.

Name

Ww  Bb

1.

2.

3.   W

4.   b

Objectives: Together with children, name each picture. Children colour pictures whose names begin with /w/ for row 1 and /b/ for row 2. For row 3, they write *w* below each picture whose name begins with /w/. Repeat for row 4 with *b*.

At-Home Activity: Say a list of words that begin with /w/ and /b/. Invite your child to wave each time you name a word that begins with the same sound as *wig* and to bend each time you name a word that begins with the same sound as *ball*.

The Letters v r j y   Vv  Rr

Roses Are Red

Roses are red,

Violets are blue,

Sugar is sweet,

And so are you.

Objectives: Children listen to the poem; circle each picture whose name begins with the same sound as *vest;* and underline each picture whose name begins with the same sound as *rabbit.* Children listen to the poem again for words that begin with /v/ and /r/.

At-Home Activity: With your child, look at home for things whose names begin with the same sound as *vest* and as *rabbit.*

Name ....

Vv 🦺 Rr 🐇

1. ▢▢▢

2. ▢▢▢

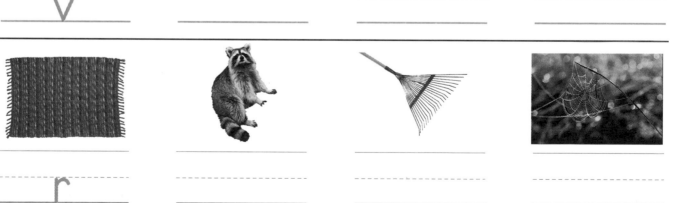

3. ▢▢▢   V

4. ▢▢▢   r

Objectives: Together with children, name each picture. Children colour pictures whose names begin with /v/ for row 1 and /r/ for row 2. For row 3, they write *v* below each picture whose name begins with /v/. Repeat for row 4 with *r*.

At-Home Activity: With your child, make up riddles whose answers begin with the same sound as *vest*. For example, *You put water and flowers in it. (vase)* Then repeat for answers that begin with the same sound as *rabbit.*

Jj  Yy

Who Took the Cookies From the Cookie Jar?

Who took the cookies
　　from the cookie jar?
Yolanda took the cookies
　　from the cookie jar.
Who me?
Yes, you!
Not me!
Then who?

Objectives: Children listen to the choral poem; circle each picture whose name begins with the same sound as *jar;* and put an X on each picture whose name begins with the same sound as *yellow.* Children listen to the choral poem again for words that begin with /j/ and /y/.

At-Home Activity: With your child, look in stores for things whose names begin with the same sound as *jar* and as *yellow.* Chant "Who Took the Cookies From the Cookie Jar?" together, replacing *Yolanda* with your names.

Jj  Yy

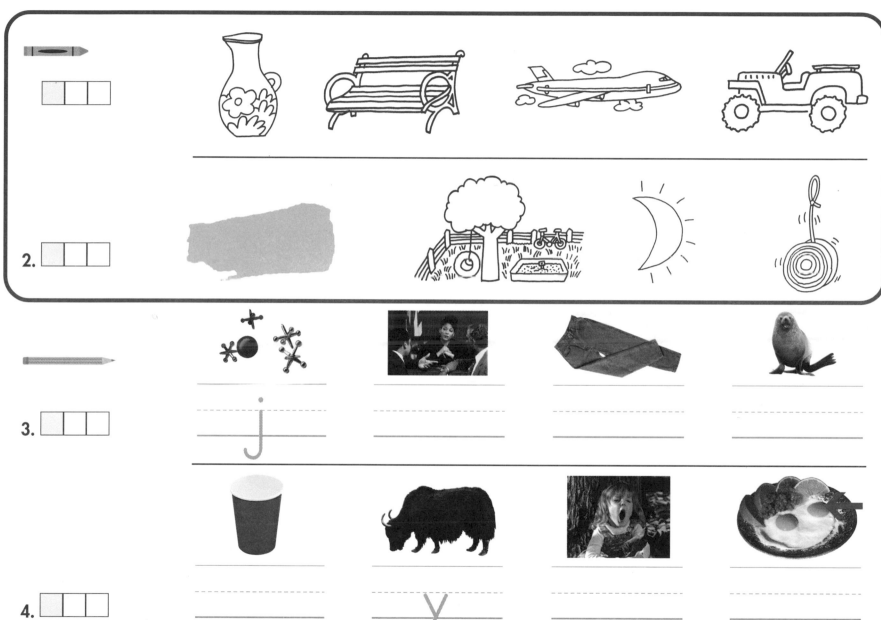

1.

2.

3. j

4. y

Objectives: With children, name each picture. Children colour pictures whose names begin with /j/ for row 1 and /y/ for row 2. For row 3, they write *j* below each picture whose name begins with /j/. Repeat for row 4 with *y*.

At-Home Activity: With your child, name family members and friends whose names begin with the same sound as *Jessie*. Together, make up tongue twisters that contain words that begin with the same sound as *yellow*. For example, *Your yellow yak yawned yesterday.*

Readiness Name ....

The Letters z g e

 Zz Gg

Come Out to Play

Goat and Goose come out
to play,
The moon is shining bright
as day.
Zebra zooms, and Gorilla
zips.
Guinea Pig zigzags, and
Seal does flips!

Objectives: Children listen to the nursery rhyme; circle each picture whose name begins with the same sound as *zipper;* and put an X on each picture whose name begins with the same sound as *gate*. Children listen to the nursery rhyme again for words that begin with /z/ and /g/.

At-Home Activity: Take turns naming words that begin with the same sound as *zipper*. With your child, look for things at home that begin with the same sound as *gate*.

Name ....

Zz  Gg

1.

2.

3. z

4. g

Objectives: With children, name each picture. Children colour pictures whose names begin with /z/ for row 1 and /g/ for row 2. For row 3, they write z below each picture whose name begins with /z/. Repeat for row 4 with g.

At-Home Activity: Write a zero each time you or your child names a word that begins with the same sound as *zero*. Ask how many zeros you wrote. Then with your child, look through magazines for pictures of things whose names begin with the same sound as *gate*.

Ee  Ed

Two Little Red Birds

Two little red birds,

Sitting on a shed.

One named Eddy,

The other named Ed.

Fly away, Eddy.

Fly away, Ed.

Come back, Eddy.

Come back, Ed.

Objectives: Children listen to the fingerplay, then circle each picture whose name has /e/ as in *net*. They listen to the fingerplay again for words that have /e/.

At-Home Activity: With your child, look for things whose names have the sound of *e* as in *Ed* and *net*.

Name

Ee Ed

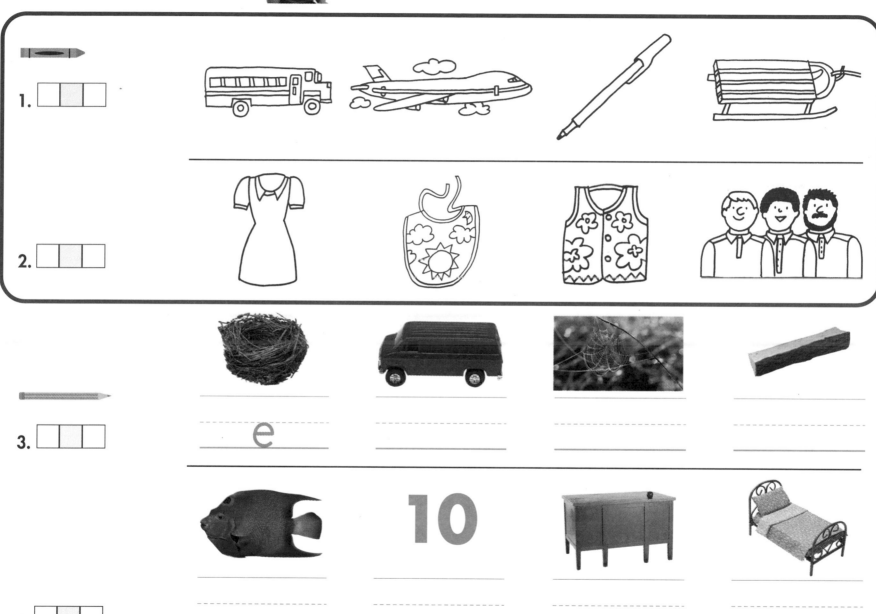

1.

2.

3. e

4.

Objectives: With children, name each picture. For rows 1 and 2, children colour each picture whose name has /e/. For rows 3 and 4, they write *e* below each picture whose name has /e/.

At-Home Activity: With your child, draw pictures of things whose names have the sound of *e* as in *Ed* and *nest*.

The Letters k q x u Kk  Qq

The Kind Kangaroo

Kind Jumpety-Bumpety-Hop-
and-Go-One
Was quietly asleep on his
quilt in the sun.
This kind kangaroo quickly
flicked the flies,
With his long glossy tail from
his ears and his eyes.
Kind Jumpety-Bumpety-Hop-
and-Go-One!

Objectives: Children listen to the poem; circle each picture whose name begins with the same sound as *king*; and underline each picture whose name begins with the same sounds as *queen*. Children listen to the poem again for words that begin with /k/ and /kw/.

At-Home Activity: With your child, look in books for pictures of things whose names begin with the same sound as *king* and as *queen*.

Name

Kk Qq

1.

2.

3.

   k

4.

   qu

Objectives: Together with children, name each picture. Children colour pictures whose names begin with /k/ for row 1 and /kw/ for row 2. For row 3, they write *k* below each picture whose name begins with /k/. Repeat for row 4 with /kw/ spelled *qu*.

At-Home Activity: Begin sentences for your child to complete with a word that begins with the same sound as *king*. For example, *I open the door with a ___. (key)* Repeat for words that begin with the same sounds as *quilt. The woman with a sparkling crown is the ___. (queen)*

Xx  **Uu**

Uncle Max

Upstairs lives our uncle
  Max Cox,
With six cats, a fox, and
  an ox.
Uncle Max told us, "I'm
  itchy,"
Then he went uptown to
  Dr. Ritchey,
Who said, "Max Cox,
  you've got chicken pox!"

Objectives: Children listen to the limerick; circle the pictures whose names end with the same sounds as *box;* and put an *X* on each picture whose name has /u/ as in *umbrella* and *tub.* Children listen to the limerick again for words with /ks/ and /u/.

At-Home Activity: With your child, draw on slips of paper pictures of things whose names end with the same sounds as *box,* and put the slips in a shoebox. Then draw an outline of a tub. Inside the outline, draw pictures of things whose names have the sound of *u* as in *umbrella* and *tub.*

Name

Xx Uu

1.

2.

6

3.

x

4.

u

Objectives: With children, name each picture. Children colour pictures whose names end with /ks/ for row 1, and whose names have /u/ as in *umbrella* and *tub* for row 2. For row 3, they write *x* below each picture whose name ends with /ks/. Repeat for row 4 for picture names with *u*.

At-Home Activity: With your child, pretend to mix batter as you take turns saying words that end with the same sounds as *mix*. Then sit down together. Stand up each time one of you says a word that has the sound of *u* as in *up* and *tub*.

Readiness Name

The Patterns -an -at -ad

Mix a Pancake

Mix a pancake,
Stir a pancake,
Pop it in the pan.

Fry the pancake,
Toss the pancake,
Catch it if you can.

Objectives: Children clap each time they hear a word in the poem that rhymes with *man*. They circle each picture whose name rhymes with *sad* and underline pictures whose names rhyme with *bat*. Then children listen to the poem again and underline each word that rhymes with *man*.

At-Home Activity: With your child, draw an outline of a large van. Inside draw pictures of things whose names rhyme with *van*. *(can, man, pan)*

1.

2.

3.

4.  m a ☐    m a ☐    m a ☐

5. c ☐ ☐    h ☐ ☐    s ☐ ☐

Objectives: Children identify the pictures in each row. They circle each picture whose name ends with the same sounds as *fan* in row 1, *cat* in row 2, and *dad* in row 3. In rows 4 and 5, children say each sound in the picture names and write the letter or letters in the boxes to complete the words.

At-Home Activity: With your child, look at a favourite picture book for objects whose names rhyme with *hat*, *fan*, and *sad*.

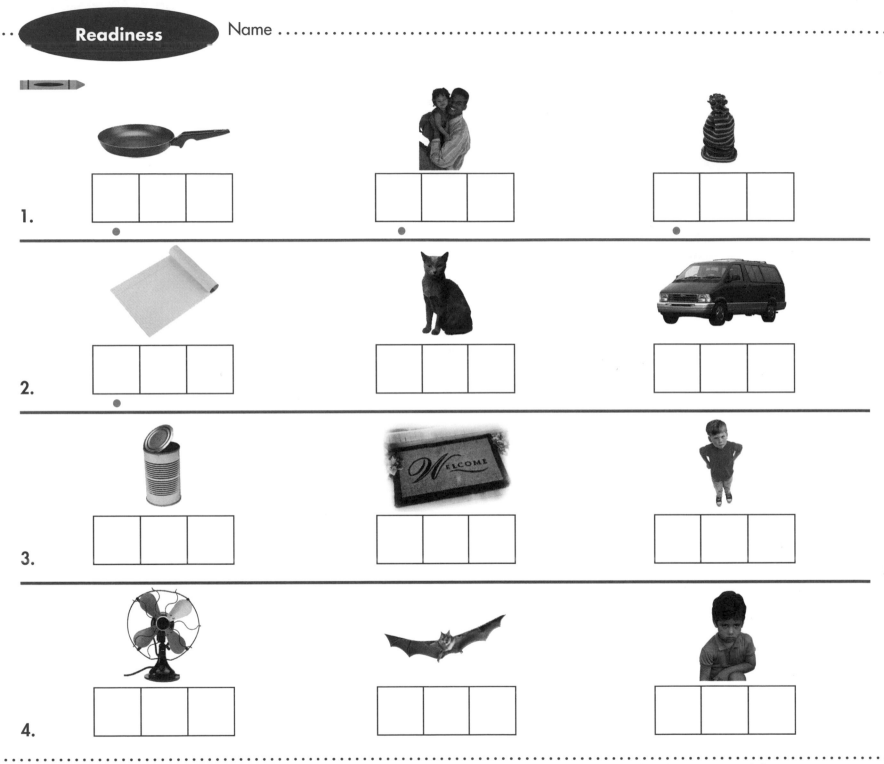

Name ....

1.

2.

3.

4.

Objectives: Children name each picture and say each sound separately. Then they hear one sound in each word and colour the corresponding box. (Picture names: *pan, dad, hat, pad, cat, van, can, mat, mad, fan, bat, sad*)

At-Home Activity: With your child, take turns naming words that rhyme with *mad*. Repeat with *pan* and *hat*.

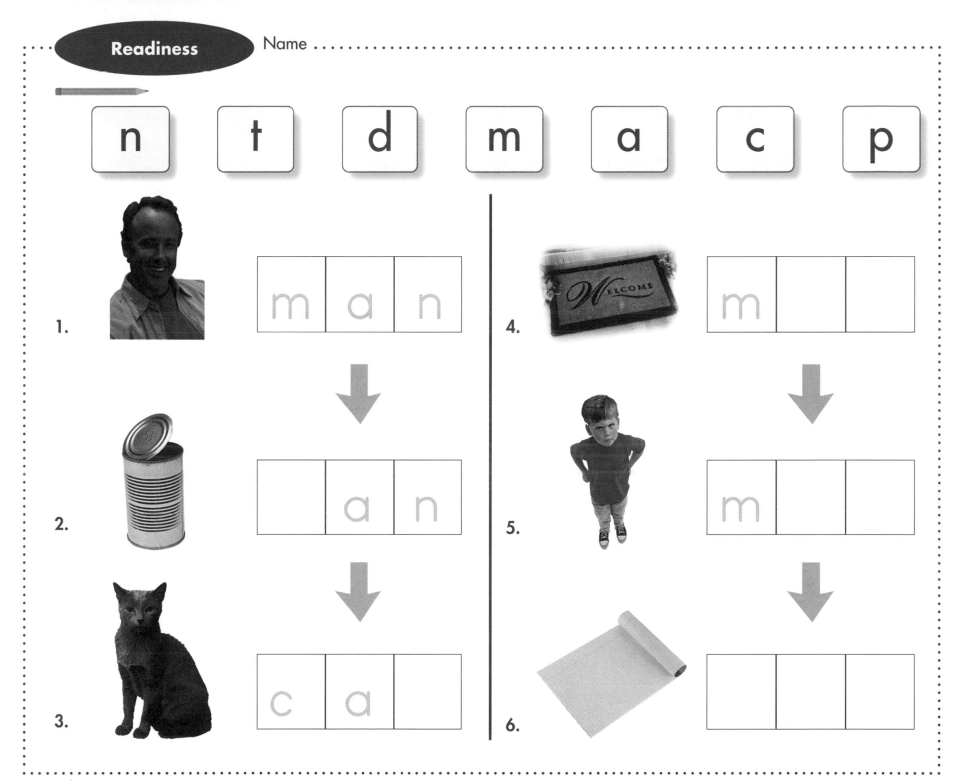

Readiness   Name ....

n   t   d   m   a   c   p

1.   m | a | n

2. | a | n

3.   c | a |

4.   m | |

5.   m | |

6. | |

Objectives: Children identify the first picture in column 1 and trace the letters for the picture name. Then they substitute letters to write a new word that names each picture. They continue in column 2 by writing phonograms to complete words before writing the entire last word.

At-Home Activity: Write the letters a, b, n, d, h, m, n, p, and t on small squares of paper. With your child, make as many -an, -at, and -ad words as you can to use the letter squares.

The Patterns -an -at -ad   **39**

LESSON 9

The Patterns -ot -op -og

Pease Porridge

Pease porridge hot,
Pease porridge cold,
Pease porridge in the pot,
Nine days old.

Some like it hot,
Some like it cold,
Some like it in the pot,
Nine days old.

Objectives: Children listen for words in the poem that rhyme with *not*. They circle each picture whose name rhymes with *hop* and underline pictures whose names rhyme with *jog*. Then children listen to the poem again and underline each word that rhymes with *got*.

At-Home Activity: Have your child listen for words that rhyme with *pot*. Say words such as *lot, pen, got, pat, rot, cot*. Your child can tap a pot for each word that rhymes with *pot*. Then have your child say words for you to tap.

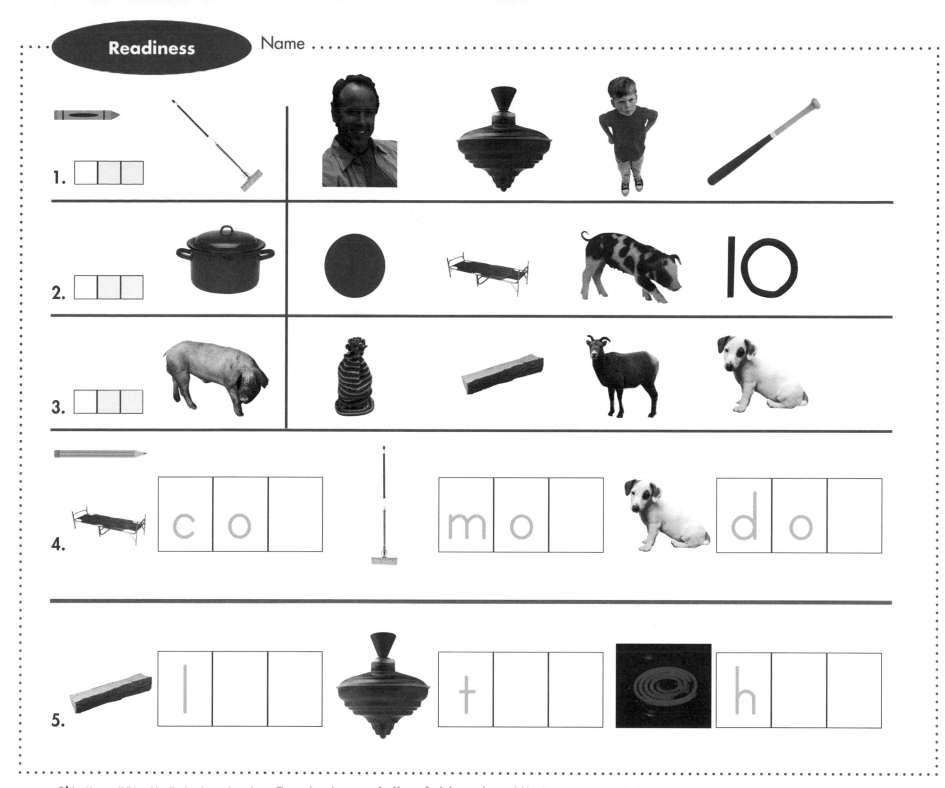

1.

2.

3.

4.   c o | m o   d o

5.   l   t   h

Objectives: Children identity the pictures in each row. They circle each picture whose name ends with the same sounds as *mop* in row 1, *pot* in row 2, and *hog* in row 3. In rows 4 and 5, children say each sound in the picture names and write the letter or letters in the boxes to complete the words.

At-Home Activity: With your child, take turns naming words that rhyme with *hop*. Repeat with *cot* and then *fog*.

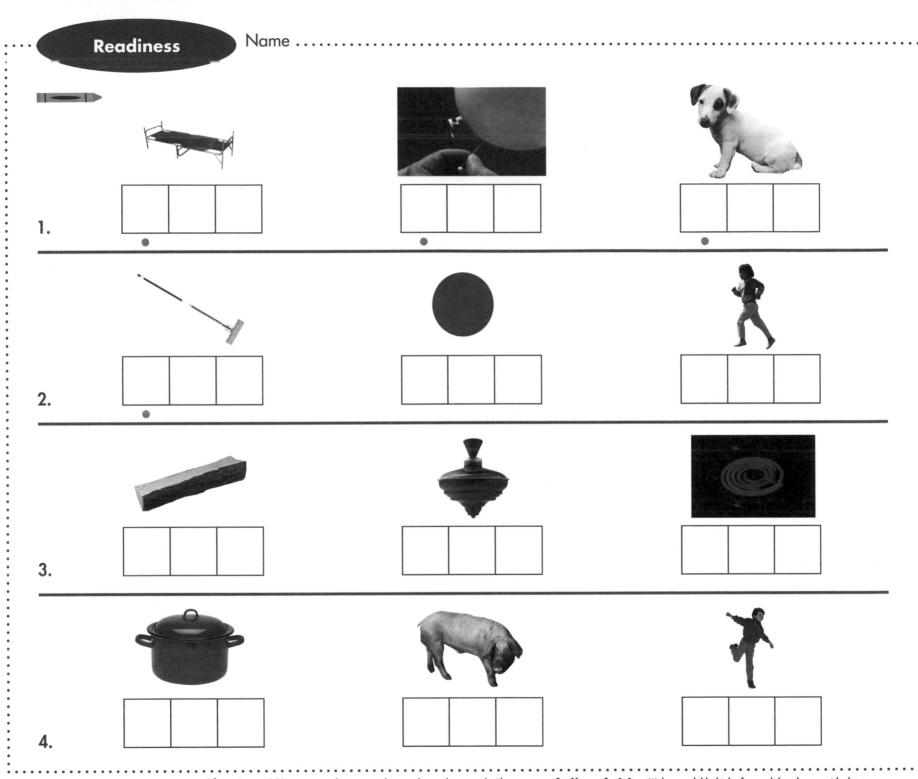

Readiness

Name ....

1.

2.

3.

4.

Objectives: Children name each picture and say each sound separately. Then they hear one of the sounds in each word and colour the corresponding box. (Picture names: *cot, pop, dog, mop, dot, jog, log, top, hot, pot, hog, hop*)

At-Home Activity: With your child, think of a word that rhymes with *dog* to make a rhyming phrase he or she can illustrate. For example, *fog dog* or *log dog.*

42 Lesson 9

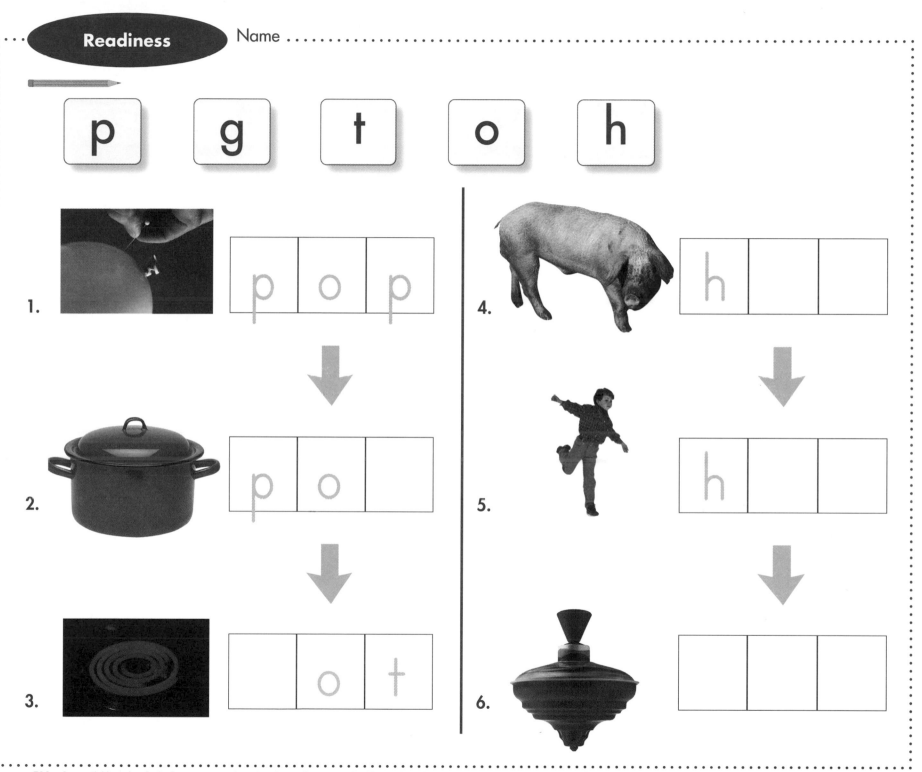

| p | g | t | o | h |

1. | p | o | p |

2. | p | o | |

3. | | o | t |

4. | h | | |

5. | h | | |

6. | | | |

Objectives: Children identify the first picture in column 1 and trace the letters for the picture name. Then children substitute letters to write a new word that names each picture. They continue in column 2 by writing phonograms to complete words before writing the entire last word.

At-Home Activity: Write the letter patterns *-ot*, *-op*, and *-og* and the letters *c, d, g, h, l, p,* and *t* on squares of paper. With your child, see how many *-ot*, *-op*, and *-og* words you can make using the letter squares.

The Patterns -ig -it -ill

August Heat

In August, when the
days are hot,
I like to find a shady
spot,
And hardly move a bit.
And sit.
And sit.
And sit.
And sit!

Objectives: Children listen for words in the poem that rhyme with *kit*. They put a circle around a picture whose name rhymes with *big* and an *X* on the picture whose name rhymes with *fill*. Then children listen to the poem again and underline each word that rhymes with *fit*.

At-Home Activity: With your child, take turns naming words that rhyme with *sit*. Make up a silly sentence, using some of the rhyming words.

1.

2.

3.

4. p i   p i   d i

5. w   s   h

Objectives: Children name the pictures in each row. They circle each picture whose name ends with the same sounds as *pig* in row 1, *kit* in row 2, and *hill* in row 3. In rows 4 and 5, children say each sound in the picture names and write the letter or letters in the boxes to complete the words.

At-Home Activity: With your child, finish a rhyme that begins *Jack and Jill*. For example, *Jack and Jill cooked dinner on the grill* or *Jack and Jill said, "Hi Bill."*

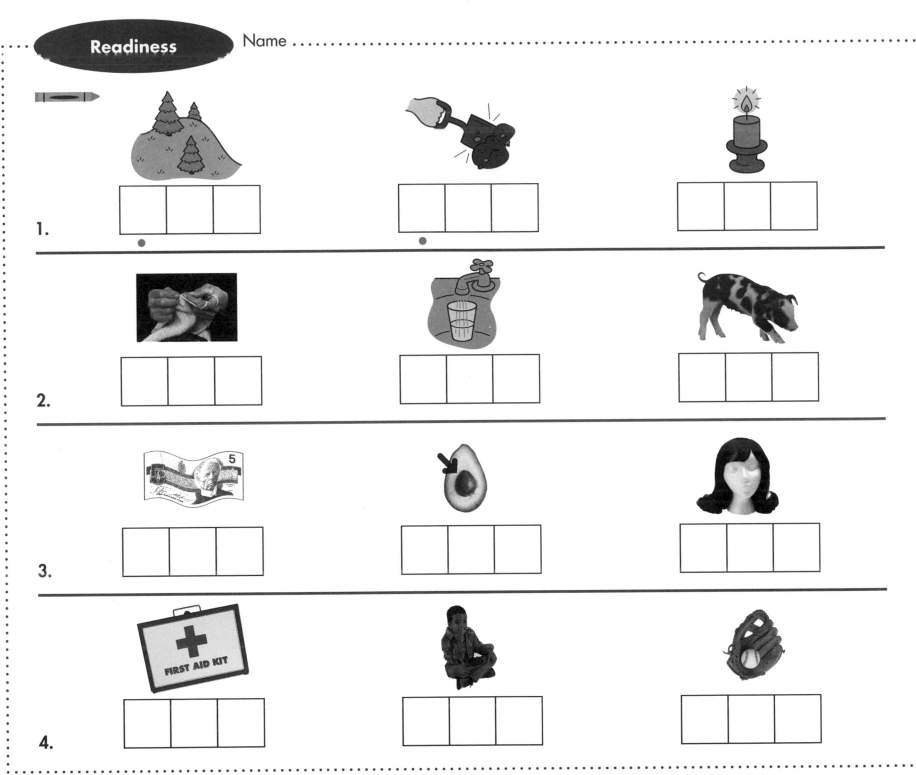

1.

2.

3.

4.

Objectives: Children listen to the name of each picture. Then they hear one of the sounds in each word and colour the corresponding box. (Picture names: *hill, dig, lit, knit, fill, pig, bill, pit, wig, kit, sit, mitt*)

At-Home Activity: Ask your child to draw a picture of a big pig. Then encourage your child to make up a sentence about the drawing.

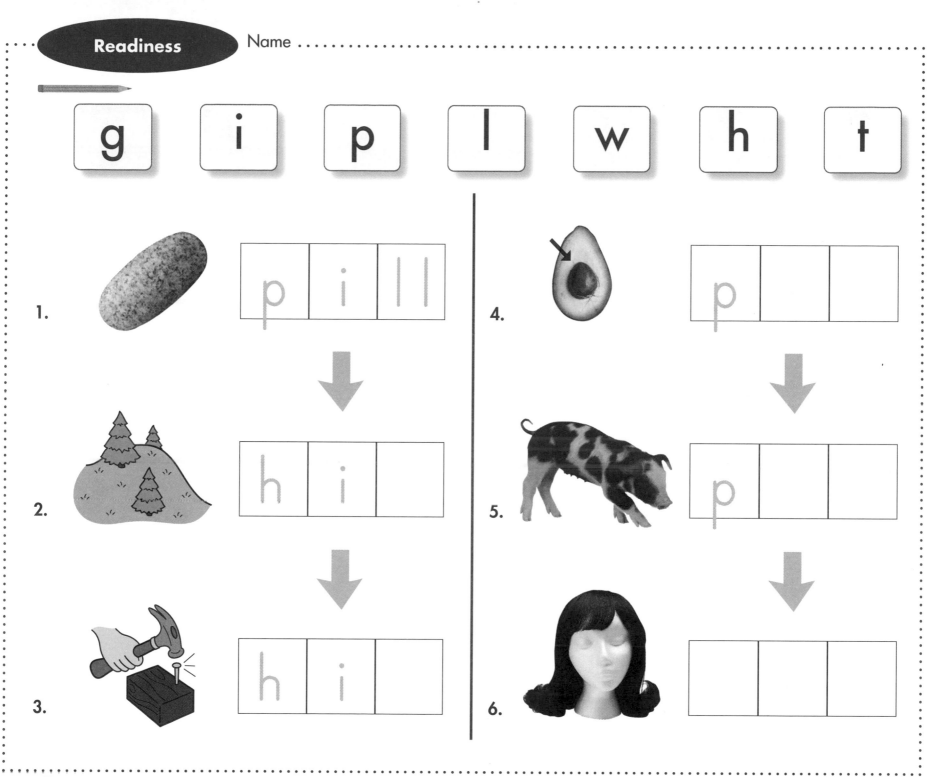

g   i   p   l   w   h   t

1.   p | i | ll

2.   h | i |

3.   h | i |

4.   p | |

5.   p | |

6. | |

Objectives: Children identify the first picture in column 1 and trace the letters for the picture name. Then children substitute letters to write a new word that names each picture. They continue in column 2 by writing phonograms to complete words before writing the entire last word.

At-Home Activity: Together, think of words that rhyme with *pill, pit,* and *pig.* (*hill, still, mill, fill, will, bit, hit, fit, sit, big, dig, fig, wig*)

The Patterns -ed -en -et

One, Two

One, two,
buckle my shoe.
Three, four,
shut the door.
Five, six,
pick up sticks.
Seven, eight,
lay them straight.
Nine, ten,
a nice fat hen.

Objectives: Children hold up ten fingers each time they hear a word in the poem that rhymes with *pen*. They circle pictures whose names rhyme with *fed*; underline pictures whose names rhyme with *get*. They listen to the poem again and underline each word that rhymes with *pen*.

At-Home Activity: With your child, find or draw pictures of a hen, a pen, and two stick-figure men. Ask your child to say the names of the pictures as you label them.

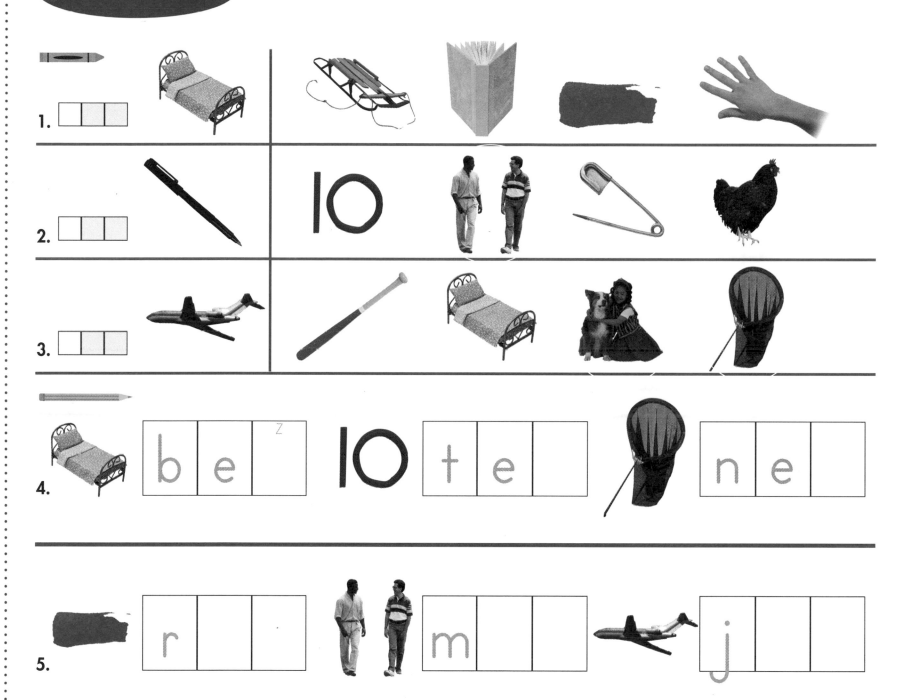

1.

2.

3.

4. be z   10 te   ne

5. r   m   j

Objectives: Children name the pictures in each row. Then they circle each picture whose name ends with the same sounds as *bed* in row 1, *pen* in row 2, and *jet* in row 3. In rows 4 and 5, children say each sound in the picture names and write the letter or letters in the boxes to complete the words.

At-Home Activity: With your child, finish a rhyme that begins *Get ready, get set.* For example, *Get ready, get set. Kick the ball in the net!*

1.

2.

3.

4.

Objectives: Children listen to the name of each picture and say each sound separately. Then they hear one of the sounds in each word and colour the corresponding box. (Picture names: *bed, hen, jet, men, fed, pet, net, ten, red, wed, wet, pen*)

At-Home Activity: With your child, make up rhymes about a boy named Ed. Use words that rhyme with his name. For example, *My friend Ed has a hat that is red.*

Name ....

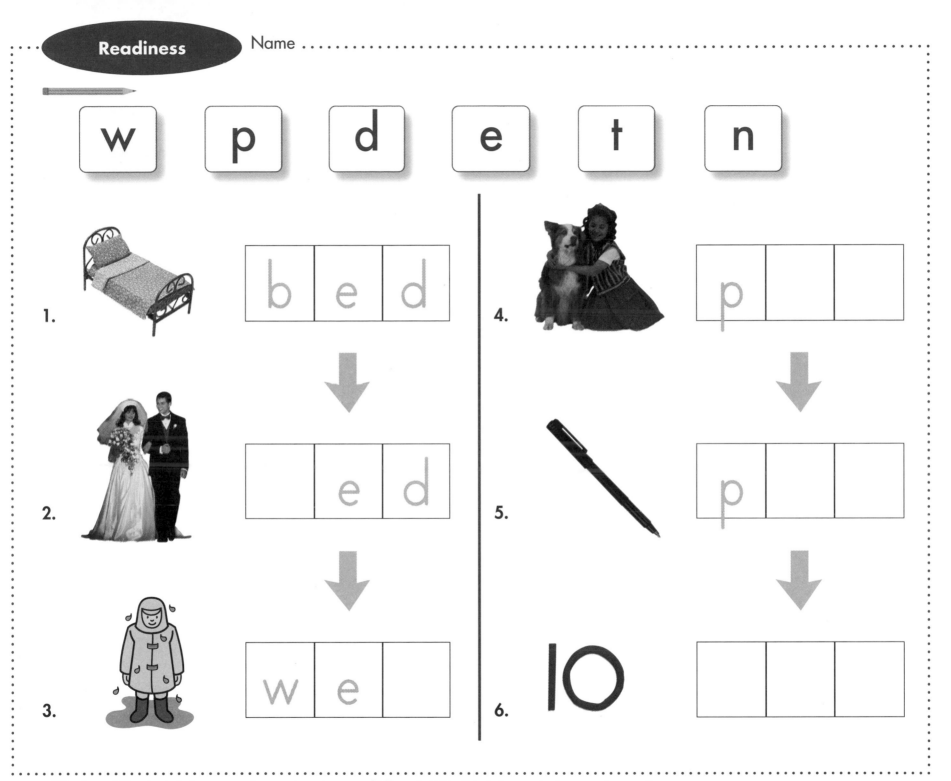

1. | b | e | d |

2. | | e | d |

3. | w | e | |

4. | p | | |

5. | p | | |

6. | | | |

Objectives: Children identify the first picture in column 1 and trace the letters for the picture name. Then children substitute letters to write a new word that names each picture. They continue in column 2 by writing phonograms to complete words before writing the entire last word.

At-Home Activity: Write the letters *b, d, e, l, m, n, p,* and *t* on small squares of paper. Together with your child, make as many *-ed, -en,* and *-et* words as you can, using the letter squares.

The Patterns   -ug   -un   -ut

Six Little Candles

Six little candles and not
 one more,
Wh! Wh! Now there are four.
Four little candles—
 red, white, and blue,
Wh! Wh! Now there are two.
Two little candles sitting
 in the sun,
Wh! Wh! It's birthday fun!

Objectives: Children clap each time they hear a word in the poem that rhymes with *bun*. They put an X on pictures whose names rhyme with *rug* and *cut*. Then children listen to the poem again and underline each word that rhymes with *run*.

At-Home Activity: Run in place with your child as you take turns naming words that rhyme with *run*. (*bun, fun, pun, sun, spun, won*)

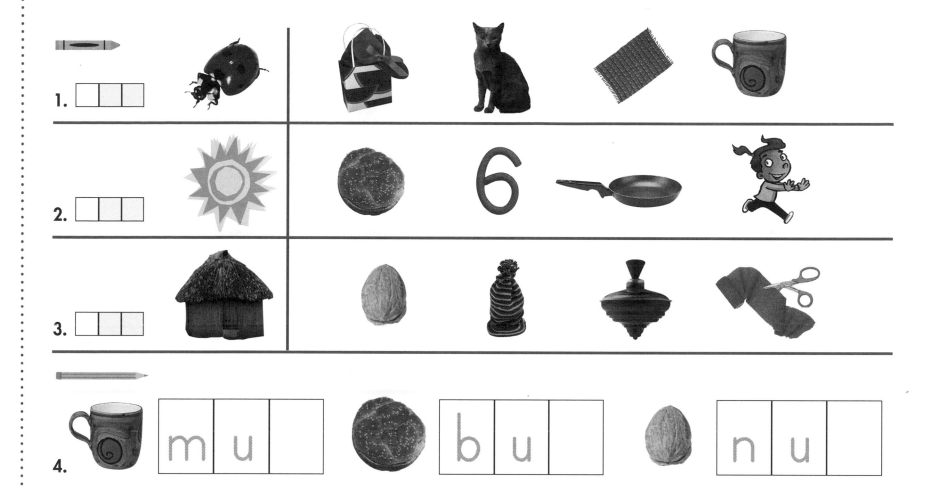

1.

2.

3.

4.

5.

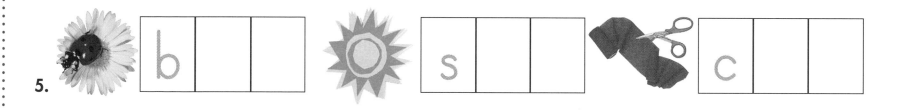

Objectives: Children name the pictures in each row. Then they circle each picture whose name ends with the same sounds as *bug* in row 1, *sun* in row 2, and *hut* in row 3. In rows 4 and 5, children say each sound in the picture names and write the letter or letters in the boxes to complete the words.

At-Home Activity: With your child, play "A-Hug-a-Word." Hug each other each time you or your child names a word that rhymes with *hug*. (*bug, dug, lug, mug, rug, tug*)

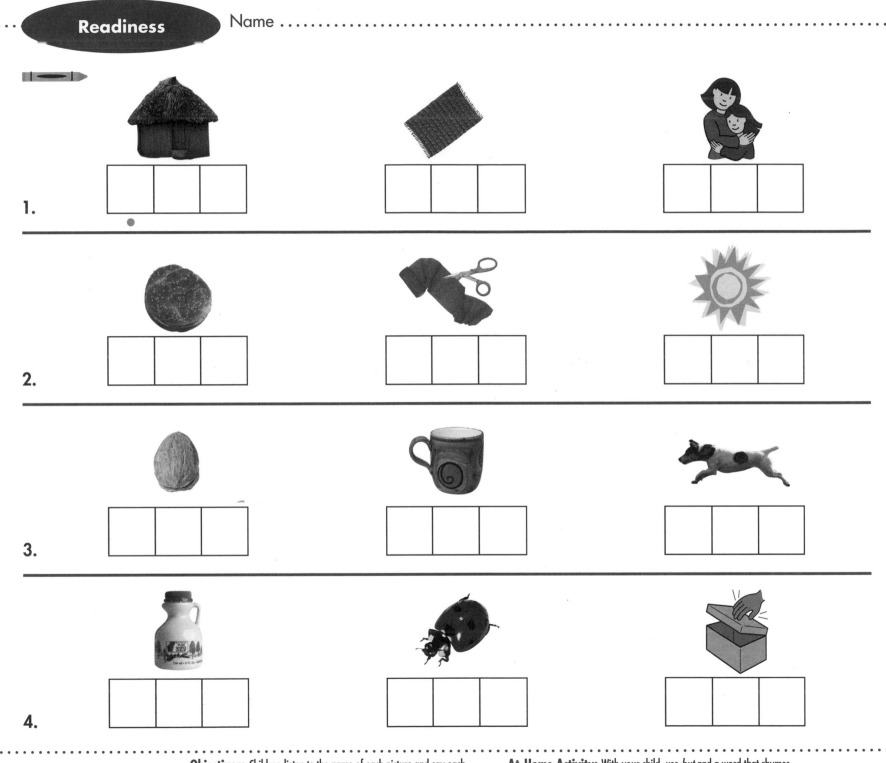

1.

2.

3.

4.

Objectives: Children listen to the name of each picture and say each sound separately. Then they will hear one of the sounds in each word and colour the corresponding box.

At-Home Activity: With your child, use *hut* and a word that rhymes with it in a question. For example, *Does a hut have a door to shut?* Repeat for *mug* and *sun*.

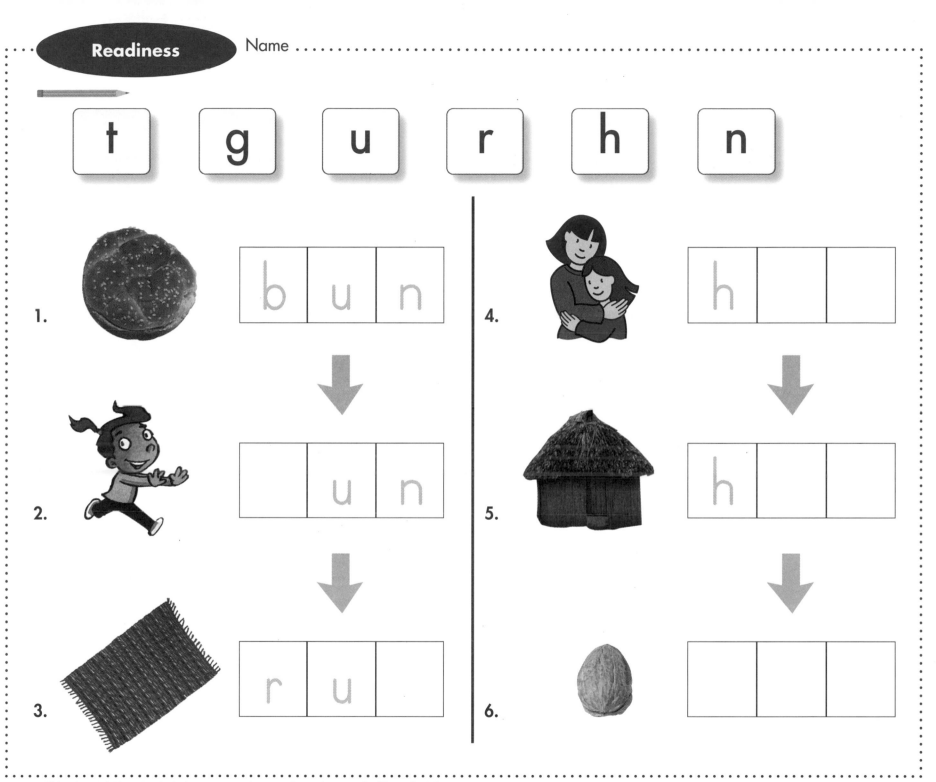

Name ....

t g u r h n

1.

| b | u | n |

↓

| | u | n |

↓

2.

| r | u | |

3.

4.

| h | | |

↓

5.

| h | | |

↓

6.

| | | |

Objectives: Children identify the first picture in column 1 and trace the letters for the picture name. Then they substitute letters to write a new word that names each picture. They continue in column 2 by writing phonograms to complete words before writing the entire last word.

At-Home Activity: Write the letters *b, g, h, j, n, r, t,* and *u* on small squares of paper. Together with your child, make as many *-ug, -un,* and *-ut* words as you can with the letter squares.

LESSON 13

Spelling Words

hat
sat
cat
can
ran
of *LOOKOUT WORD*

Learn and Spell   Name ....

Words With -at and -an

● **See and Say**    cat can
hat ran

▲ **Sounds and Letters**

-at	-an
1. _____	4. _____
2. _____	5. _____
3. _____	6. _____ *LOOKOUT WORD*

■ **Write and Check**

What happened when the cat saw the dog?

7. The cat _____ .

Objectives: Children recognize spelling patterns in words with /a/ as in *cat* and *can;* spell the high-frequency word *of;* write each spelling word.

At-Home Activity: Ask your child to name other words with *-at* and *-an .* Together, look for *-at* and *-an* words on signs or in books.

Name . . . .

● Say and Write

Say each picture name.
What spelling word begins the same way?

1. _____

2. _____

3. _____

4. _____

5. _____

▲ Work With Rhymes

Write the missing spelling words.
Circle the words that rhyme.

6. This fat _____ is Nat.

7. Jan has a can _____.

8. Nat _____ on the _____.

Word Hunt
Look outside on signs for -at and -an words.

SPELL CHAT

What little word is in **cat**? in **can**?

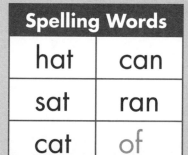

Spelling Words	
hat	can
sat	ran
cat	of

Objectives: Children write the spelling words that begin like picture names. They write spelling words to complete sentences and circle rhyming words.

At-Home Activity: With your child, find objects with -at and -an names, such as mat, hat, and can. Use notes to label each object.

Words With -at and -an   57

Name

Spelling Words

hat
sat
cat
can
ran
of

Quick Write

Write about a funny thing a cat can do. Use two spelling words. Begin with a capital letter.

● **Write Words**

Tell about the picture.
Write the missing spelling words.

1. The cat _____ play a game.

2. The _____ hides a hat.

3. Can the dog find the _____?

▲ **Proofread**

Jamie found one word she spelled wrong.
Circle three more words spelled wrong.
Write the words on the lines.

4. _____

5. _____

6. _____

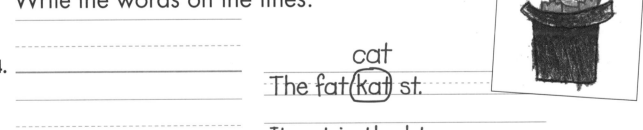

cat
The fat (kat) st.

It sat in the ht.

The cat kan hide.

Jamie

Objectives: Children write spelling words to complete sentences and proofread written work.

At-Home Activity: Help your child write a sentence about a funny thing a cartoon cat did. Together, proofread for spelling and capital letters.

Use ABC Order
Write the missing letters in ABC order.

1. W _____ _____

2. _____ e _____

3. _____ _____ o

Test Yourself

Trace	Copy	Cover and Write
4. hat		
5. sat		
6. cat		
7. can		
8. ran		
9. of		

For Tomorrow

⟹ See the word.

◇ Say it slowly.

☐ Link sounds and letters.

▽ Write.

⬤ Check.

Share What -at and -an words did you find?

Objectives: Children write letters in alphabetical order and self-test by tracing, copying, and then writing from memory each spelling word.

At-Home Activity: Help your child get ready for the spelling test by giving him or her a practice test.

Spelling Words

had

sad

bad

bag

wag

the

Name ....

Words With -ad and -ag

● **See and Say**

had   bag
sad   wag

▲ **Sounds and Letters**

-ad	-ag
1. _____	4. _____
2. _____	5. _____
3. _____	6. _____

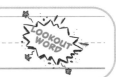

■ **Write and Check**

Write the missing spelling words. Then
say the sentence as fast as you can.

7. The _____ ate a _____ of .

Objectives: Children recognize spelling patterns in words with /a/ as in
had and *bag*; spell the high-frequency word *the*; and write each spelling word.

At-Home Activity: Ask your child to name other words with *-ad* and
-ag. Together, look for *-ad* and *-ag* words on cards and notes.

Word Practice

Name . . . .

● **Say and Write**

Say each picture name. Write the spelling word that begins the same way.

1. _____ad

2. _____ad

3. _____ag

4. _____ag

5.  _____ad

▲ **Work With Words**

Write the missing spelling words.

6. Tag looks _____.

7. Dan has _____  in a _____.

8. A big tail will _____.

Objectives: Children build and then write spelling words. They write spelling words to complete sentences.

At-Home Activity: Take turns asking and answering riddles with your child. Use spelling words. For example, *What is tan and can wag?* (dog)

Name . . . .

Spelling Words

| had |
| sad |
| bad |
| bag |
| wag |
| the |

Quick Write

Write a list of three things a dog or cat does. Use one spelling word.

● Write Words

Change one letter in **sat**. Write a spelling word.

1. _____

Change one letter in **bat**. Write two spelling words.

2. _____ 3. _____

▲ Proofread

Ali found one word she spelled wrong. Circle three more words spelled wrong. Write the words on the lines.

4. _____

5. _____

6. _____

The (Bd) Bad Snow
A man hd to get food.

Tan ran fast.

Tan got th bg of food.

Ali

Objectives: Children manipulate letters to write spelling words and proofread written work.

At-Home Activity: Empty a bag such as a schoolbag or laundry bag. Help your child write a sentence that begins *In the bag we had* . . . .

Name ....

● Use ABC Order

Write the missing letters in ABC order.

1. _____ b _____   2. i _____ _____   3. _____ _____ u

▲ Test Yourself

Trace	Copy	Cover and Write
4. had		
5. sad		
6. bad		
7. bag		
8. wag		
9. the		

For Tomorrow

⬜➡ See the word.

◇ Say it slowly.

☐ Link sounds and letters.

▽ Write.

⬣ Check.

Share What -ad and -ag words did you find?

Name . . . .

Words With -op and -ot

● **See and Say**

hop   hot

top   not

▲ **Sounds and Letters**

-ot	-op
1. _____	4. _____
2. _____	5. _____
3. _____	6. _____ LOOKOUT WORD

Spelling Words

top
hop
hot
got
not
and *LOOKOUT WORD*

■ **Write and Check**

How does a bear feel when it rolls in the snow?

7. _____ _____

Objectives: Children recognize spelling patterns in words with /o/ as in *hop* and *hot*; spell the high-frequency word *and*; and write each spelling word.

At-Home Activity: Help your child find *-op* and *-ot* words on store signs and in shop windows.

Word Practice

Name . . . .

● Say and Write

Put together a letter from a red train car with
letters from a yellow train car. Say the words.
Write the ones that are spelling words.

1. _____   2. _____   3. _____

▲ Work With Words

Look at each picture.
Write the missing spelling word.

4. "I _____ !"

5. "I am _____ !"

6. "I got a dog _____ a cat."

Word Hunt
Look at signs for -op and
-ot words, such as **Stop**
or **Hot Soup**.

SPELL CHAT

Name three words that
rhyme with **got**.

Spelling Words	
top	got
hop	not
hot	and

Objectives: Children write spelling words by adding -op and -ot to initial
consonants and write spelling words to complete sentences about pictures.

At-Home Activity: Help your child add consonants such as *l*, *m*, or *p*
to -op and -ot to create more words. (*lot, pot, mop, pop*)

Name . . . .

Spelling Words

top
hop
hot
got
not
and

Quick Write

Write an animal tale. Use two spelling words. End each sentence with a period.

● **Write Words**

Finish the rabbit tale. Write spelling words.

1. The 🐰 will _____ up the hill.

2. He will hop to the_____.

3. He _____ a 🎀.

▲ **Proofread**

Tom found one word he spelled wrong.
Circle three more words spelled wrong.
Write the words on the lines.

4. _____

5. _____

6. _____

and
The Cat (anb) Top

The cat gt a top.

The tp did nit go.

Tom

Objectives: Children write words to complete a tale and proofread written work.

At-Home Activity: Have your child use spelling words to write a sentence about something that hops. Proofread for spelling and end punctuation.

Use ABC Order

Write the missing letters in ABC order.

1. d _____ _____ _____ g _____   2. _____ _____ m _____ o _____

▲ Test Yourself

Trace	Copy	Cover and Write
3. top		
4. hop		
5. hot		
6. got		
7. not		
8. and		

Objectives: Children write letters in alphabetical order and self-test by tracing, copying, and then writing from memory each spelling word.   **At-Home Activity:** Help your child get ready for the spelling test by giving a practice test.

Words With -op and -ot   67

For Tomorrow

➡ See the word.

◇ Say it slowly.

☐ Link sounds and letters.

▽ Write.

⬡ Check.

Share What -op and -ot words did you find?

Learn and Spell

Name .....

Words With -og

● **See and Say**

dog   log
fr(og)   f(og)

Spelling Words

dog
frog
log
hog
fog
I LOOKOUT WORD

▲ **Sounds and Letters**

-og

1. _____   4. _____

2. _____   5. _____

3. _____   6. _____ LOOKOUT WORD

■ **Write and Check**

What did the little frog say to the big frog?

7. Don't _____ the _____!

Objectives: Children recognize the spelling pattern -og as in dog and log; spell the high-frequency word I; and write each spelling word at least once.

At-Home Activity: Help your child scan posters on the street and in stores for -og words and the word I.

● Say and Write

Say each picture name.
Write the spelling word that goes with it.

1. _____

2. _____

3. _____

4. _____

Say the picture name.
Write the spelling word
that sounds the same.

5. _____

▲ Work With Words

Write spelling words in the sentences.

6. The _____ and
the _____ can jog.

7. They jog in the _____!

Objectives: Children use picture clues to write the spelling words; name a picture word; and write spelling words to complete sentences.

At-Home Activity: Ask your child a question, using spelling words. For example: *Is the hog lost in the fog?* Help your child answer, using spelling words.

Word Hunt

Look at posters for -og words and the word **I**.

SPELL CHAT

Name four words that begin like **hog**.

Spelling Words	
dog	hog
frog	fog
log	I

Spelling Words

dog
frog
log
hog
fog
I

Quick Write
Write about a dog or frog. Use two spelling words and a capital **I**.

● **Write Words**
Use spelling words to finish the story.

1. I am a _____ .

2. _____ sit on a _____ .

3. _____ hide in the _____ .

▲ **Proofread**
Nora found one word she spelled wrong.
Circle three more words spelled wrong.
Write the words on the lines.

4. _____

5. _____

6. _____

I
Ⓘ can see the frg.
She is hiding in the lg.
Will the dg find her?

Nora

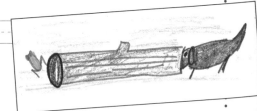

Objectives: Children write spelling words to complete a story and proofread written work.

At-Home Activity: Encourage your child to draw a picture of a dog and then to write and proofread a sentence about the drawing.

Name ....

● Use ABC Order

Write the missing letters in ABC order.

1. e ____ ____ h ____   2. ____ o p ____ ____

▲ Test Yourself

Trace	Copy	Cover and Write
3. dog		
4. frog		
5. log		
6. hog		
7. fog		
8. I		

For Tomorrow

⟹ See the word.

◇ Say it slowly.

☐ Link sounds and letters.

▽ Write.

⬣ Check.

Share What -og words did you find?

Objectives: Children write letters in alphabetical order and self-test by tracing, copying, and then writing from memory each spelling word.

At-Home Activity: Help your child get ready for the spelling test by giving him or her a practice test.

LESSON 17

Spelling Words

sit
fit
hit
hid
did
they *LOOKOUT WORD*

Words With -it and -id

● **See and Say**   s|it   d|id
f|it   h|id

▲ **Sounds and Letters**

-it	-id
1. _____	4. _____
2. _____	5. _____
3. _____	6. _____ *LOOKOUT WORD*

■ **Write and Check**

Write the missing spelling words that rhyme.

7. Can he _____ and _____?

Objectives: Children recognize spelling patterns in words with /i/ as in *sit* and *hit*; spell the word *they*; and write each spelling word at least once.

At-Home Activity: Help your child find and read *-it* and *-id* words in a favourite storybook.

Name ....

● Say and Write

Write the missing spelling words in the riddles.

1. What did the ball ask the bat?

   _____ you _____ me?

2. What has legs but does not stand?

Two dogs that _____.

▲ Work With Rhymes

Write the missing spelling words.
Circle the words that rhyme.

3. _____ will play.

4. He _____ under the lid.

5. Will it _____?

SPELL CHAT

Name three words that end like **hit**.

Spelling Words	
sit	hid
fit	did
hit	they

Objectives: Children say and write spelling words to complete and answer riddles; write spelling words that rhyme; and circle rhyming words.

At-Home Activity: With your child, talk about games children play. Try to use each spelling word.

Spelling Words

sit
fit
hit
hid
did
they

Quick Write

Write about a ball game. Use two spelling words.

● **Write Words**

Change one letter at the beginning of **hit**.
Make two spelling words.

1. _____ 2. _____

Now change the last letter of **hit**.
Then change the first letter of the new word.

3. _____ 4. _____

▲ **Proofread**

Josh found one word he spelled wrong.
Circle two more words spelled wrong.
Write the words on the lines.

5. _____

6. _____

They

(Thay) will play.

Kit ht the ball.

Dad bid not get it.

Wag did.

Josh

Objectives: Children change beginning and ending letters in the word *hit* to write other spelling words and proofread written work.

At-Home Activity: Ask your child to write two short sentences using the spelling words. Help your child proofread his or her work.

Study and Review Name ....

Use ABC Order

Write these letters in ABC order.

1. **s h d** _____

2. **t b m** _____

3. **g v e** _____

▲ Test Yourself

Trace	Copy	Cover and Write
4. sit		
5. fit		
6. hit		
7. hid		
8. did		
9. they		

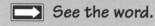

For Tomorrow

 See the word.

◇ Say it slowly.

☐ Link sounds and letters.

▽ Write.

⬡ Check.

Share What -it and -id words did you find?

Objectives: Children write words in alphabetical order and self-test by tracing, copying, and then writing from memory each spelling word.

At-Home Activity: Help your child get ready for the spelling test by giving him or her a practice test.

Name...

Write a Frog and Dog Poem

Write the missing words.
Make a poem.

The _____ can run.
(1)

The frog can _____.
(2)

Just for some fun,

_____ dog _____ run
(3) (4)

With the _____ on top!
(5)

can   dog

the   frog

hop

Objectives: Children write spelling words to complete a poem.

At-Home Activity: Ask your child to name the frog and the dog and to create another poem about the funny duo.

76   Lesson 18

Name ....

Word Puzzles

Fill in the missing letters.
Make spelling words.

had   bag   hop
got   hid   did

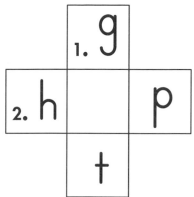

1. g
2. h   p
   t

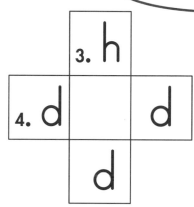

3. h
4. d   d
   d

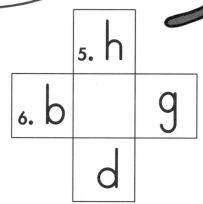

5. h
6. b   g
   d

What words are in the puzzles?
Write them on the lines.

1. _____

2. _____

3. _____

4. _____

5. _____

6. _____

Objectives: Children fill in crossword puzzles with vowels to make spelling words and write the spelling words.

At-Home Activity: Write *hat* and ask your child to change one letter at a time to make new words. For example, *pat*, *pan*, and *tan*.

hop   frog

I   and

they   bag

of   sit

Name ....

● **What Is It?**
Read each clue.
Write the spelling word.

1. You can put things in it. _____

2. It likes to hop. _____

3. You call yourself this. _____

4. You do this on one leg. _____

▲ **Make It Rhyme**
Name the picture word.
Write the spelling word that rhymes.

5. _____

6. _____

7. _____

8. _____

Objectives: Children write spelling words that match clues and write spelling words that rhyme with picture names.

At-Home Activity: With your child, make up a clue for one of the spelling words. Help your child write the clue and the answer.

Write the Missing Word
Read each sentence.
Fill in the correct word.

Read Jen's message to Bob.

1. I had a _____ of _____.
   big
   bag

2. The _____ ate one.
   dog
   log

3. The _____ ate two.
   fog
   frog

4. I _____ and ate.
   cat
   sat

5. I _____ the rest.
   had
   bad

6. _____ you want one?
   did
   dad

Dear Bob,
I hd the bag.
From,
Jen

Bob thought I **had** the bag. I really **hid** the bag!

Objectives: Children complete sentences with the correct spelling words.

At-Home Activity: Say messages with spelling words, leaving out each spelling word. For example, *I walked the ____.* (dog) Ask your child to complete the message.

Name ....

Words With -in and -ig

Spelling Words

win
pin
pig
big
dig
are LOOKOUT WORD

● **See and Say**

w in   p ig

p in   d ig

▲ **Sounds and Letters**

-ig	-in
1. _____	4. _____
2. _____	5. _____
3. _____	6. _____ LOOKOUT WORD

■ **Write and Check**

How can the pig get out of the sun?

7. The _____ can _____.

Objectives: Children recognize spelling patterns in words with /i/ as in *win* and *pig*; spell the high-frequency word *are*; and write each spelling word.

At-Home Activity: Play Simon Says, using *-in* words. For example, *Simon says spin around.* Ask your child to repeat the *-in* word.

● **Say and Write**
Finish the riddle. Fill in the missing spelling words.

1. Why does the pig _____ ?

2. The _____ thinks it is a dog!

▲ **Work With Words**
Write the missing spelling words.

3. The dog is _____ .

4. The pigs _____ little.

5. Who will _____ the _____ ?

Word Hunt
Listen to your friends.
List -in words you hear.

SPELL CHAT

What little word is in **win**?

Spelling Words	
win	big
pin	dig
pig	are

Objectives: Children write spelling words to complete a riddle and to complete sentences.

At-Home Activity: With your child, use as many spelling words as you can to create silly sentences. For example, *The pig can win a big wig.*

Spelling Words

win
pin
pig
big
dig
are

Quick Write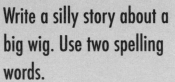
Write a silly story about a big wig. Use two spelling words.

● **Write Words**
Use spelling words to finish the story.

1. The _____ and _____ race.

2. The pig will _____ the race.

3. He can win a _____.

▲ **Proofread**
Carrie found one word she spelled wrong.
Circle three more words spelled wrong.
Write the words on the lines.

4. _____

5. _____

6. _____

         pig

The (peg) and the dog ar

at the house. The pig looks

in. The dog looks in.

Thay see a bg cat.   Carrie

Objectives: Children write spelling words to complete a story and proofread written work.

At-Home Activity: Help your child use spelling words to write a sentence about a pig. Together, proofread for spelling and punctuation.

Name ....

● Use ABC Order
Write these letters in ABC order.

1. **w p b**

2. **x f n**

3. **s y g**

▲ Test Yourself

Trace	Copy	Cover and Write
4. win		
5. pin		
6. pig		
7. big		
8. dig		
9. are		

Share What -in and -ig words did you find?

Objectives: Children write letters in alphabetical order and self-test by tracing, copying, and then writing from memory each spelling word.

At-Home Activity: Help your child get ready for the spelling test by giving him or her a practice test.

LESSON 20

Spelling Words

fill
hill
spill
still
will
you 

Words With -ill

● **See and Say**

f**ill**   sp**ill**
h**ill**   st**ill**

▲ **Sounds and Letters**

-ill

1. _____

2. _____

3. _____

4. _____

5. _____

6. _____

■ **Write and Check**

What will happen if Jack trips?

7. The water _____ _____ !

Objectives: Children recognize spelling patterns in words with *ill*, as in *fill*; spell the high-frequency word *you*; and write each spelling word.

At-Home Activity: Together, make up nonsense rhymes with the spelling words and other words ending in *-ill*.

Name . . . .

● Say and Write

Say each picture name.
What spelling word begins the same way?

1. 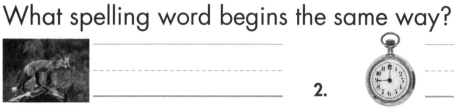 _____

2. _____

3. _____

4. _____

▲ Work With Words

Write the missing spelling words in the poem.

Be quiet, Bill.

5. Be very _____.

6. If the  wakes up, _____ will take a _____!

Objectives: Children write spelling words that begin with the same sounds as the picture names, and write spelling words to complete the poem.

At-Home Activity: With your child, take turns pantomiming some spelling words. For example, *fill* a glass with milk.

Word Hunt

Look at signs to find -ill words.

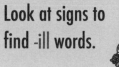

SPELL CHAT

What are two names that rhyme with **hill**?

Spelling Words	
fill	still
hill	will
spill	you

Name . . . .

Spelling Words

fill
hill
spill
still
will
you

Quick Write

Write a two-line poem and a title. Use two spelling words.

⬤ **Write Words**

Write spelling words to finish the poem.

1. Will Jack go up a _____?

2. He has a pail to _____.

3. Jill said, "He _____."

▲ **Proofread**

Ellen found one word she spelled wrong. Circle three more words spelled wrong. Write the words on the lines.

4. _____

5. _____

6. _____

The Cat and the Hog
                    ran
The hog (rn) up the hil.

The cat hab a spil.

                    Ellen

Objectives: Children write spelling words to complete a poem and proofread written work.

At-Home Activity: With your child, write a new title for the poem about the cat and the hog. Capitalize each important word.

● Use ABC Order

Write these letters in ABC order.

1. **S W F**

2. **T P C**

3. **O D H**

▲ Test Yourself

Trace	Copy	Cover and Write
4. fill		
5. hill		
6. spill		
7. still		
8. will		
9. you		

Objectives: Children write letters in alphabetical order and self-test by tracing, copying, and then writing from memory each spelling word.

At-Home Activity: Support your child by giving him or her a practice spelling test.

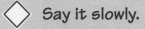
For Tomorrow

 See the word.

◇ Say it slowly.

□ Link sounds and letters.

▽ Write.

● Check.

Share What -ill words did you find?

LESSON 21

Spelling Words

let

get

pet

ten

hen

with LOOKOUT WORD

Words With -et and -en

● **See and Say**

g(et)   t(en)

p(et)   h(en)

▲ **Sounds and Letters**

-et	-en
1. _____	4. _____
2. _____	5. _____
3. _____	6. _____ LOOKOUT WORD

■ **Write and Check**

What will happen when you give your dog a bath?

7. Your _____ will _____ wet.

Objectives: Children recognize spelling patterns in words with /e/ as in *let* and *ten*; spell the high-frequency word *with*; and write each spelling word.

At-Home Activity: Ask your child to name other words with *-et* and *-en*. Together, look for *-et* and *-en* words on signs or food containers.

● Say and Write

Say the spelling word that answers each riddle. Then write it.

1. You get eggs from me.
   I rhyme with **ten**.   _____

2. You give me food.
   I rhyme with **get**.   _____

3. I come after nine.
   I rhyme with **men**.   _____

▲ Work With Words

Write spelling words that fit in the boxes.

4. _____

5. _____

6. _____

Word Hunt
Look for -et and -en words on your way to school.

SPELL CHAT

Name other words that fit in the same boxes.

Spelling Words	
let	ten
get	hen
pet	with

Spelling Words

let
get
pet
ten
hen
with

Quick Write

Write a question about a pet. Don't forget the question mark. Use two spelling words.

● **Write Words**

Write spelling words to name each picture.

1.  _____

2. _____

3.  _____

▲ **Proofread**

Fumi found one word he spelled wrong in his wish list. Circle three more words spelled wrong. Write the words on the lines.

4. _____

5. _____

6. _____

_____ Fumi
get
I want to (gat) a pet.

I would lt you play

woth her.

Do yu like cats?

Objectives: Children write words that name things they see in the pictures and proofread written work.

At-Home Activity: Ask your child to write a question about a wish. Help your child proofread his or her work and include a question mark.

● Use ABC Order

Write each set of letters in ABC order.

1. **n l k m**
   _____
   - - - - - - - - - - - -
   _____

2. **s r u t**
   _____
   - - - - - - - - - - - -
   _____

3. **h e g f**
   _____
   - - - - - - - - - - - -
   _____

▲ Test Yourself

Trace	Copy	Cover and Write
4. let		
5. get		
6. pet		
7. ten		
8. hen		
9. with		

For Tomorrow

⇨ See the word.

◇ Say it slowly.

☐ Link sounds and letters.

▽ Write.

⬡ Check.

Share What -et and -en words did you find?

Objectives: Children write letters in alphabetical order and self-test by tracing, copying, and then writing from memory each spelling word.

At-Home Activity: Help your child get ready for the spelling test by giving him or her a practice test.

Words With *-et* and *-en*   91

Spelling Words

leg
beg
bed
fed
red
for 

Words With -ed and -eg

● **See and Say**

bed   leg

red   beg

▲ **Sounds and Letters**

-ed	-eg
1. _____	4. _____
2. _____	5. _____
3. _____	6. _____ 

■ **Write and Check**

How can you tell when the dogs want to nap?

7. The dogs_____ at the_____.

Objectives: Children recognize spelling patterns in words with /e/ as in *leg* and *bed*; spell the high-frequency word *for*; and write each spelling word.

At-Home Activity: Label two envelopes *-eg* and *-ed*. Help your child write *-eg* and *-ed* words on cards and store them in the correct envelope.

● Say and Write

Say the child's name. Change the first letter
to write spelling words.

Ted   **Meg**

1. _____   3. _____

2. _____   4. _____

▲ Work With Words

Finish the story with spelling words.
Circle two pairs of words that rhyme.

5. Ned saw spots of _____.

6. Ned had to go to _____.

7. Mama got a book _____ him.

Word Hunt
Look in stores for
-eg and -ed words.

SPELL CHAT

Change one letter in **bed**.
Make a new spelling word.
What is it?

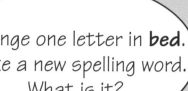

Spelling Words	
leg	fed
beg	red
bed	for

Objectives: Children substitute initial consonants to write picture
names that rhyme and write spelling words to complete a story.

At-Home Activity: Using spelling words, make up a simple two-line
poem with your child.

Words With *-ed* and *-eg*   93

Spelling Words

leg
beg
bed
fed
red
for

Quick Write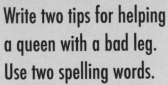
Write two tips for helping a queen with a bad leg. Use two spelling words.

● **Write Words**

Finish the story. Use spelling words.

"How to Wake a Prince"

1. Ring the _____ bell.

2. _____ _____ help.

▲ **Proofread**

Tara found one word she spelled wrong. Circle three more words spelled wrong. Write the words on the lines.

3. _____

4. _____

5. _____

Tara   for
How to Care (fr) a Queen

1. Put Queen Meg in bd.

2. Help her lig rest.

3. Give her tea wth milk.

Objectives: Children write spelling words to complete a story and proofread written work.

At-Home Activity: With your child, take turns naming a person or pet you have fed. Then help your child write a sentence such as *I fed Tan.*

● Use ABC Order

Write the missing letters in ABC order.

1. _____ i j _____   2. t _____ _____ w   3. k _____ m _____

▲ Test Yourself

Trace	Copy	Cover and Write
4. leg		
5. beg		
6. bed		
7. fed		
8. red		
9. for		

For Tomorrow

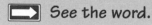 See the word.

◇ Say it slowly.

☐ Link sounds and letters.

▽ Write.

⬣ Check.

Share What -eg and -ed words did you find?

Objectives: Children write letters in alphabetical order and self-test by tracing, copying, and then writing from memory each spelling word.

At-Home Activity: Help your child get ready for the spelling test by giving him or her a practice test.

Name . . . .

Words With -ug and -ut

● **See and Say**   b|ug| b|ut|
                    h|ug| c|ut|

Spelling Words
hug
rug
bug
but
cut
one *LOOKOUT WORD*

▲ **Sounds and Letters**

-ug	-ut
1. _____	4. _____
2. _____	5. _____
3. _____	6. *LOOKOUT WORD* _____

■ **Write and Check**

What is it when a fly's wings are around you?

7. a _____

Objectives: Children recognize spelling patterns in words with /u/ as in *bug* and *but*; spell the high-frequency word *one*; and write each spelling word.

At-Home Activity: Help your child make up riddles for *-ug* and *-ut* words. For example, Name of a cozy insect? *(a snug bug)*

Name . . . .

● Say and Write

Read each sentence. Write the missing letters. Then write the spelling words.

1. A b___g is on the r___g.

_____ _____

_____ _____

2. B___t I can get it! _____

▲ Work With Words

Write the missing spelling word.
Circle the words that name more than one.

3. one _____  two hugs

4. one _____  two cuts

5. _____ _____ two bugs

Word Hunt
Look at directions for -ug and -ut words.

SPELL CHAT

What letter do you add to a word to make it tell about more than one?

Spelling Words	
hug	but
bug	cut
rug	one

Objectives: Children write spelling words to complete sentences; use picture clues to write spelling words; and identify plural nouns.

At-Home Activity: Encourage your child to draw and label pictures of one bug or cut, and two or more bugs or cuts.

Spelling Words

hug
rug
bug
but
cut
one

Quick Write

Write something about yourself. Use two spelling words.

● **Write Words**

Write the missing spelling words.

1. I like to _____.

2. I like the _____.

3. I like the big _____.

▲ **Proofread**

Russ found one word he spelled wrong. Circle three more words spelled wrong. Write the words on the lines.

4. _____

5. _____

6. _____

bug

I have wun pet (buk.)

I let the bug on the rg.

I ded not let him on the bed.

Russ

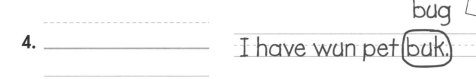

Objectives: Children use picture clues to write words to complete a story and proofread written work.

At-Home Activity: With your child, choose something he or she does well. Help him or her write one or two sentences about it.

Name . . . .

For Tomorrow

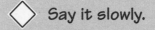 See the word.

◇ Say it slowly.

☐ Link sounds and letters.

▽ Write.

⬡ Check.

● Use ABC Order

Write these letters in ABC order. **b r h o**

1. _____   2. _____   3. _____   4. _____

▲ Test Yourself

Trace	Copy	Cover and Write
5. hug		
6. rug		
7. bug		
8. but		
9. cut		
10. one		

Share What -ug and -ut words did you find?

Objectives: Children write letters in alphabetical order and self-test by tracing, copying, and then writing from memory each spelling word.

At-Home Activity: Help your child get ready for the spelling test by giving him or her a practice test.

Name ....

Rhyme Time

Write the missing words.
They rhyme with the underlined words.

big   still

win   ten

get   bed

1. A _____ pig has a wig.

2. Bill is _____ here.

3. Let the pet _____ wet.

4. Fred has a red _____ .

5. A hen sees _____ men.

6. A thin man will _____ .

Objectives: Children complete sentences by writing spelling words that rhyme with underlined words in the sentences.

At-Home Activity: Have your child write spelling words that rhyme with *wig, pet,* and *hen.*

Name ....

Picture Rhymes

Circle the picture name.
Then write the spelling word
that rhymes with it.

win	will	beg
fed	hug	but

1. fin   pin   _____

2. peg   leg   _____

3. fill   hill   _____

4. bed   red   _____

5. rug   bug   _____

6. hut   nut   _____

Objectives: Children circle the word that names the picture and write the spelling word that rhymes with the picture name.

At-Home Activity: With your child, play the "Rhymes-With" game. Take turns calling out words that rhyme with *win, fed,* and *but.*

Name ....

Find the Secret Words

Use the code to write spelling words.
A picture stands for each missing letter.

w   f   r   y   h   n   t

1. o u _____

2. i _____

3. o e _____

4. a e _____

5. o _____

6. e _____

are   for

ten   one

with   you

Objectives: Children write spelling words, using a code for letters.

At-Home Activity: Ask your child to read the decoded words aloud. Help your child write *win*, using the code.

Name ....

Write the Right Word
Read the pairs of sentences.
Finish them with the correct word.

Read Nan's note to her new friend.

hug   hog

1. This is a _____.

2. He is hard to _____.

bag   big

3. The box is _____.

4. Can it fit in the _____?

but   bat

5. He has a _____.

6. He plays, _____ he is out!

Dear Sari,
My hen sits all
day. She sits on
tn eggs.
Your pal,
Nan

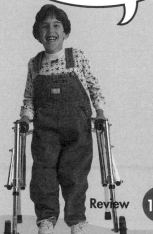

Sari thought my hen has **tan** eggs. The hen really has **ten** eggs!

Objectives: Children write spelling words to complete sentence pairs.

At-Home Activity: With your child, make up a pair of sentences for *beg* and *bed*. Encourage your child to write the sentences and then illustrate them.

Name . . . .

LESSON 25

Spelling Words

fun
sun
run
rub
tub
is 

Words With -un and -ub

● **See and Say**

r⟨u⟩n   r⟨u⟩b
f⟨u⟩n   t⟨u⟩b

▲ **Sounds and Letters**

-un	**-ub**
1. _____	4. _____
2. _____	5. _____
3. _____	6. _____ 

■ **Write and Check**

What did the cloud say to chase the sun away?

" _____ _____ !"

7. _____ , _____ .

Objectives: Children recognize spelling patterns in words with /u/ such as *run* and *rub*; spell the high-frequency word *is*; and write each spelling word.

At-Home Activity: Help your child make a chart with the headings *-un* and *-ub*. Invite him or her to name *-un* and *-ub* words and record them.

● Say and Write

Look at the letters in each sun. Fill in the letters to write the spelling words below.

un   ub   r

1. t ___ ___

2. f ___ ___

3. s ___ ___

4. ___ u b

5. ___ u n

▲ Work With Words

Write spelling words on the lines. Circle the words that rhyme.

Rub a dub dub,

6. A dog in a ____ .

7. This ___ not ____ .

8. Look at him ____ !

SPELL CHAT

What word is a number, rhymes with **fun**, but has no letter **u**?

Spelling Words	
fun	rub
sun	tub
run	is

Objectives: Children write letters to finish spelling words and write spelling words to complete a poem.

At-Home Activity: With your child, use spelling words and rhyming words to make up sentences. Your child can illustrate a sentence.

Name . . . .

Spelling Words

fun
sun
run
rub
tub
is

Quick Write

Write about a game.
Use two spelling
words. Write **I** with
a capital letter.

● **Write Words**

Write the missing spelling words.

1. The _____ ___ hot.

2. Dad fills the _____.

3. We _____ the cars.

▲ **Proofread**

Gus found one word he spelled wrong.
Circle three more words spelled wrong.
Write the words on the lines.

4. _____

5. _____

6. _____

fun

I read for (fon.)

Then I rn in the hot sen.

I run with my bg dog.

Gus

Objectives: Children write spelling words to complete a description and
proofread written work.

At-Home Activity: Ask your child to use spelling words to write one
or two sentences describing something fun. Help your child proofread.

Name ....

● Use ABC Order

Write these words in ABC order.　**sun　fun　run**

1. _____

2. _____

3. _____

▲ Test Yourself

Trace	Copy	Cover and Write
4. fun		
5. sun		
6. run		
7. rub		
8. tub		
9. is		

At-Home Activity: Help your child get ready for the spelling test by giving him or her a practice test.

For Tomorrow

→ See the word.

◇ Say it slowly.

□ Link sounds and letters.

▽ Write.

● Check.

Share What -un and -ub words did you find?

Spelling Words

make
take
came
ate
late
read  LOOKOUT WORD

Name . . . .

Words With a-e

● **See and Say**

make   came
take   late

▲ **Sounds and Letters**

-ake	-ate	-ame
1. _____	3. _____	5. _____
2. _____	4. _____	6. _____ LOOKOUT WORD

■ **Write and Check**

Was Snail on time?

7. He _____ _____ .

Objectives: Children recognize long *a* words with the *a-e* pattern; spell the high-frequency word *read;* and write each spelling word.

At-Home Activity: Write a note to your child, using an *a-e* word. For example, *Please make your bed.* Help your child write a note back to you.

Name . . . .

● Say and Write

What spelling word finishes each sentence?
Write the word.

1. They _____ the pie.

2. Jo and Pam _____ the pie.

3. The pets _____ the pie.

▲ Work With Verbs

Look at the underlined words below.
Then write spelling words on the lines.

4. Dad and I <u>made</u> soup.

You can _____ it, too.

5. We <u>took</u> some to Mike.

You can _____ some, too.

Objectives: Children write spelling words to complete sentences about pictures and write present-tense verbs in sentences.   **At-Home Activity:** With your child, hold a conversation in which each of you uses at least one spelling word in every sentence.

Word Hunt

Look in store windows for a-e words such as **take**.

SPELL CHAT

Make has an **m** and **take** has a **t**. How are they the same?

Spelling Words	
make	ate
take	late
came	read

Spelling Words

make

take

came

ate

late

read

Quick Write

Write a poem about a person or animal you like. Use two spelling words.

● **Write Words**

Use spelling words to finish the poem.

1. Tom came _____ with a cake.

2. Sam _____ with a big snake!

▲ **Proofread**

Kate found one word she spelled wrong.
Circle three more words spelled wrong.
Write the words on the lines.

3. _____

4. _____

5. _____

Kate

Jake and Jane
                is
Jake (iz) at the gate.

What plane did he tak?

Jane kame lat.

Objectives: Children write words to complete a poem and proofread written work.

At-Home Activity: Help your child use spelling words and rhyming words to write a poem. Help proofread spelling and capital letters.

Name ....

● Use ABC Order

Write these words in ABC order.   **make   came   late**

1. _____

2. _____

3. _____

▲ Test Yourself

Trace	Copy	Cover and Write
4. make		
5. take		
6. came		
7. ate		
8. late		
9. read		

For Tomorrow

▭➡ See the word.

◇ Say it slowly.

▢ Link sounds and letters.

▽ Write.

⬡ Check.

Share What a-e words did you find?

Objectives: Children write words in alphabetical order and self-test by tracing, copying, and then writing from memory each spelling word.

At-Home Activity: Help your child get ready for the spelling test by giving him or her a practice test.

Words With *a-e*   **111**

LESSON 27

Spelling Words

hope
home
rode
nose
those
has LOOKOUT WORD

Learn and Spell   Name ....

Words With o-e

● **See and Say**   hope rode home those

▲ **Sounds and Letters**

-ope

1. _____

-ode

4. _____

-ose

2. _____

3. _____

-ome

5. _____

6. _____ LOOKOUT WORD

■ **Write and Check**

What did the nose say to the rose?

7. A _____ can't talk!

Objectives: Children recognize long *o* in words with the *o-e* spelling pattern; spell the high-frequency word *has;* and write each spelling word.

At-Home Activity: Work with your child to find *o-e* words in magazine and newspaper ads.

● Say and Write

Finish the sentences. Write spelling words that rhyme with the underlined words.

1. The <u>toad</u> _____ .

2. A <u>rose</u> is by my _____ .

3. <u>Close</u> _____ windows!

4. I _____ I can jump <u>rope</u>.

▲ Work With Words

Read what the elephants say. Look at the underlined words. Write spelling words that can mean the same thing.

5. _____

6. _____

Bill <u>owns</u> a bike.

It is at his <u>house</u>.

Word Hunt
Look in magazines for o-e words.

SPELL CHAT

Which are the only two spelling words that rhyme?

Spelling Words

hope	nose
home	those
rode	has

Spelling Words

hope
home
rode
nose
those
has

Quick Write

Write two signs. Make one a question. Use two spelling words.

● Write Words

Write spelling words to finish the sign.

1. Nice _____ for sale.

2. It _____ a big pond!

▲ Proofread

Cole found one word he spelled wrong.
Circle three more words spelled wrong.
Write the words on the lines.

3. _____

4. _____

5. _____

Home
Our (Hom)

We hop you like it.

Keep your noze up.

Do you need a

swimming cap?

Gt one here.

Objectives: Children write the spelling words that complete the sign and then proofread written work.

At-Home Activity: Ask your child a question, using some spelling words. For example, *Who has a home in a nest?* Help your child illustrate the answer.

Use ABC Order
Write these words in ABC order.   **hope   rode   nose**

1. _____   2. _____   3. _____

▲ Test Yourself

Trace	Copy	Cover and Write
4. hope		
5. home		
6. rode		
7. nose		
8. those		
9. has		

Objectives: Children write words in alphabetical order and self-test by tracing, copying, and then writing from memory each spelling word.

At-Home Activity: Help your child get ready for the spelling test by giving him or her a practice test.

For Tomorrow

⇨ See the word.

◇ Say it slowly.

▢ Link sounds and letters.

▽ Write.

⬣ Check.

Share What o-e words did you find?

Spelling Words

mine

like

hide

ride

time

her

Name ....

Words With i-e

● **See and Say**

mine hide
time ride

▲ **Sounds and Letters**

-ide

1. _____

2. _____

-ike

3. _____

-ine

4. _____

-ime

5. _____

6. _____

■ **Write and Check**

What can fly but has no wings?

7. _____

Objectives: Children recognize long *i* words with the *i-e* spelling pattern; spell the high-frequency word *her*; and write each spelling word.

At-Home Activity: Help your child find *i-e* words the next time you ride on a bus or in a car.

Name ....

● Say and Write

Change the words in the boxes to tell about now. Write spelling words.

_____

1. [rode] Change **o** to **i**. _____

_____

2. [hid] Add an **e**. _____

_____

3. [liked] Take off the **d**. _____

▲ Work With Sentences

Use the numbers to find the letters. Write the spelling words.

1	2	3	4	5	6	7	8	9
d	e	h	i	m	n	r	v	t

_____

4. The secret place is **5 4 6 2**. _____

_____

5. You won't find it in **9 4 5 2**. _____

_____

6. Tell **3 2 7** if you find it. _____

Word Hunt
Look for i-e words in the playground or park.

SPELL CHAT

What are two words that rhyme with **mine**?

Spelling Words	
mine	ride
like	time
hide	her

Objectives: Children change past-tense verbs into present-tense spelling words and write spelling words, using a code.

At-Home Activity: Talk about what you and your child will do tomorrow. Use some of the spelling words.

Spelling Words

mine
like
hide
ride
time
her

Quick Write

Write about a special time with a friend. Use two or more spelling words.

● **Write Words**
Write the missing spelling words.

1. "I _____ to _____."

2. "They won't find me this _____."

▲ **Proofread**
Darren found one word he spelled wrong.
Circle three more words spelled wrong.
Write the words on the lines.

3. _____

4. _____

5. _____

like
I (liek) my rd bike.

I rid it all the tym.

Darren

Objectives: Children write spelling words to complete sentences and proofread written work.

At-Home Activity: Ask your child what he or she likes to do. Encourage your child to write a sentence that begins with *I like*.

● Use ABC Order
Write these words in ABC order. **like   ride   hide**

1. _____   2. _____   3. _____

▲ Test Yourself

Trace	Copy	Cover and Write
4. mine		
5. like		
6. hide		
7. ride		
8. time		
9. her		

For Tomorrow

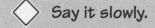 See the word.

◇ Say it slowly.

□ Link sounds and letters.

▽ Write.

⬡ Check.

Share What i-e words did you find?

Objectives: Children write words in alphabetical order and self-test by tracing, copying, and then writing from memory each spelling word.

At-Home Activity: Help your child get ready for the spelling test by giving him or her a practice test.

Spelling Words

be
he
she
me
we
his 

Words With e

● **See and Say**

be   he

me   she

▲ **Sounds and Letters**

e

1. _____ 4. _____

2. _____ 5. _____

3. _____ 6. _____

■ **Write and Check**

Who can be silly?

7. She can _____ silly.

Objectives: Children recognize spelling patterns in words with long e as in *be*; spell the high-frequency word *his*; and write each spelling word.

At-Home Activity: Together, look for the words *be, he, she, me,* and *we* in your mail or on messages and notes.

Word Hunt
Look in books at home
for e words like **he**
and **she**.

● **Say and Write**
Make new words with **e**.
Say the new word. Then write it.

1. Change the **w** in **we** to **h**. _____

2. Change the **h** in **he** to **b**. _____

3. Add an **s** before the **h** in **he**. _____

▲ **Work With Verbs**
Write the missing spelling words. Circle the
words that tell about past time.

4. _____ called Ruff.

5. He looked at ____.

6. He waited for ____ dish.

SPELL CHAT

Name two
spelling words
that begin alike.

Spelling Words	
be	me
he	we
she	his

Objectives: Children substitute letters in words to write spelling words; write spelling words to complete sentences; and circle past-tense verbs.

At-Home Activity: With your child, take turns using spelling words in sentences that tell about something that already happened.

Words With e   **121**

Spelling Words

be
he
she
me
we
his

Quick Write
Write about a place you and a friend like to go. Use two spelling words.

● **Write Words**

Look at each picture.
Write a spelling word to tell **who**.

1. _____

2. _____

3. _____

4. _____

▲ **Proofread**

Lee found one word he spelled wrong.
Circle three more words spelled wrong.
Write the words on the lines.

5. _____

6. _____

7. _____

his
Jim shared (hs) toys with mee.

Wi wanted to go to

Green Park bt it rained.

Lee

Objectives: Children write words that tell who they see in pictures and proofread written work.

At-Home Activity: Ask your child to write a sentence about the place where your family lives. Help your child proofread his or her work.

Name . . . .

Use ABC Order

Write the spelling words in ABC order.   **me   be   he**

1. _____   2. _____   3. _____

Test Yourself

Trace   Copy   Cover and Write

4. be

5. he

6. she

7. me

8. we

9. his

Objectives: Children write spelling words in alphabetical order and self-test by tracing, copying, and then writing from memory each spelling word.

At-Home Activity: Help your child get ready for the spelling test by giving him or her a practice test.

For Tomorrow

→ See the word.

◇ Say it slowly.

□ Link sounds and letters.

▽ Write.

⬡ Check.

Share What e words did you find?

Name..

What Are They Thinking?

Read what Jan and Rob are thinking.
What words are missing? Write them on the lines.

make   is

fun   she

he   her

I will have (1) with Rob.
(2) will not find me here.
I will not (3) a sound.

I know where Jan (4) .
I see (5) red .
(6) is behind that tree!

1. _____

2. _____

3. _____

4. _____

5. _____

6. _____

Objectives: Children write spelling words to complete sentences.

At-Home Activity: Ask your child to describe where Rob hides while Jan looks for him. Invite your child to write the words *he* and *she* on word cards.

124

Name ....

● Word Sets

Read the sets of words.
Write a spelling word that
has the same vowel sound.

came   rub
home

hug fun	name ate	nose rode
1. _____	2. _____	3. _____

▲ Add a Letter

Read each dark word.
Add one letter to make a spelling word.

| she | rode | his | has | read | ride |

as	is	rod
4. _____	5. _____	6. _____

rid	red	he
7. _____	8. _____	9. _____

Objectives: Children write the spelling word that has the same vowel sound as each word set and add letters to words to write spelling words.

At-Home Activity: Help your child write a sentence that uses the spelling word *rode, read,* or *rub.*

Name . . . .

● **Tell Who Rides**

Make the sentences tell about the picture. Pick the missing words. Write them on the lines.

his   she
her   he

1. ＿＿ bike is red. ＿＿＿＿＿

2. ＿＿ bike is blue. ＿＿＿＿＿

3. ＿＿ rides up. ＿＿＿＿＿   4. ＿＿ rides down! ＿＿＿＿＿

▲ **Tell About Dogs**

like   rub   we

Write the missing words on the lines.

How to Make a Dog's Tail Wag

5. You ＿＿ the dog's head. ＿＿＿＿＿＿＿＿

6. Dogs ＿＿ that! ＿＿＿＿＿＿＿＿

7. ＿＿ like that, too! ＿＿＿＿＿＿＿＿

Objectives: Children write spelling words to complete sentences that tell about a picture and write spelling words in context.

At-Home Activity: Ask your child to write *she* in the sentence *She likes her bike.* Repeat with *he* and *He likes his bike.*

Name ....

Write the Right Word

Finish each sentence.
Write the correct word.

Read Ted's sign.

Pat,

Meg is in the

park. Meet here

at 12:00.

Ted

1. Bo and Ben are _____. **has home**

2. She can _____. **ride rub**

3. He can _____ a cake. **make made**

4. Mouse _____ there. **came can**

5. What does he _____? **is like**

Pat thought my note said to meet Meg **here.** Meg wanted Pat to meet **her** at the park.

Objectives: Children write spelling words to complete sentences.

At-Home Activity: Ask your child to answer question 5 above. Together, write a sentence about what Mouse likes to do. Complete this sentence: *Mouse likes to _____.*

LESSON 31

Spelling Words

see

tree

sleep

meet

green

out

Words With ee

● **See and Say**

see   sleep
tree   meet

▲ **Sounds and Letters**

ee

1. _____   4. _____

2. _____   5. _____

LOOKOUT WORD

3. _____   6. _____

■ **Write and Check**

What is green and rhymes with **see**?

_____

7. a _____

Objectives: Children recognize spelling patterns in words in which long *e* is spelled *ee*; spell the high-frequency word *out*; and write each spelling word.

At-Home Activity: Take turns playing "Can You See . . . ," spotting things whose names have the long *e* sound.

● **Say and Write**

What letters are missing? Write the spelling word.

1. Where will we ☐eet? _____

2. We will meet at the ☐☐ee. _____

3. I have a ☐☐ee☐. _____

▲ **Rhyming Words**

Write spelling words to finish the question and answer. Circle two words that rhyme.

4. Were you _____ all day?

5. Where did you _____?

6. You can _____ me.

Word Hunt
Look in the grocery store for ee words.

SPELL CHAT

What are three words that begin like **green**?

Spelling Words	
see	meet
tree	green
sleep	out

Objectives: Children find missing letters to write spelling words; complete sentences with spelling words; and circle words that rhyme.

At-Home Activity: With your child, use spelling words to create *I see* sentences, naming the things you can see.

Words With *ee*   129

Spelling Words

see
tree
sleep
meet
green
out

Quick Write
Write about a place you like. Use two or more spelling words.

Write and Proofread   Name

● **Write Words**
Write about what you see.
Use some spelling words.

1. I _____ a house.

2. It is big and _____.

▲ **Proofread**
Lee found one word she spelled wrong.
Circle three more words spelled wrong.
Write the words on the lines.

3. _____
   _____

4. _____
   _____

5. _____

green
I like this big (gren) tre.

The dogs slep under it.

The birds have fn in it.

Lee

Objectives: Children write spelling words to describe a place and proofread written work.

At-Home Activity: With your child write a description of another place, using some of the spelling words.

● Use ABC Order

Write these words in ABC order.   **out   sleep   meet**

1. _____   2. _____   3. _____

▲ Test Yourself

Trace	Copy	Cover and Write
4. *see*		
5. *tree*		
6. *sleep*		
7. *meet*		
8. *green*		
9. *out*		

For Tomorrow

➡ See the word.

◇ Say it slowly.

□ Link sounds and letters.

▽ Write.

⬣ Check.

Share What ee words did you find?

LESSON 32

Spelling Words

eat
clean
neat
team
meat
give LOOKOUT WORD

Name . . . .

Words With ea

● **See and Say**

eat   team

meat   clean

▲ **Sounds and Letters**

-eat	ea
1. _____	4. _____
2. _____	5. _____
3. _____	6. _____ LOOKOUT WORD

■ **Write and Check**

What do you call nine baseball players who play in the rain?

7. a _____   _____

Objectives: Children recognize patterns in words in which long *e* is spelled *ea*; spell high-frequency word *give*; and write each spelling word.

At-Home Activity: With your child, name other words with *ea*. Together, look for words in menus, recipes, or supermarket flyers.

Word Practice Name . . . .

Say and Write

Write the spelling word that tells about each picture.

 1.  _____

2.  _____

3. _____

4.  _____

Work With Words

Write the missing spelling words.

5. Our room is _____.

6. Our room is _____.

7. Now we can _____.

Word Hunt
Look at store and street signs for *ea* words.

SPELL CHAT

Which spelling word rhymes with **seen**?

Spelling Words	
eat	team
clean	meat
neat	give

Words With *ea* **133**

Spelling Words

eat
clean
neat
team
meat
give

Quick Write
Write a note asking a question. Use two spelling words.

Write and Proofread Name . . . . .

● **Write Words**

Write the missing spelling words.

1. How does a _____ a ?

2. First, she must _____ it.

3. Then, she can _____ it.

▲ **Proofread**

Jan found one word she spelled wrong.
Circle three more words spelled wrong.
Write the words on the lines.

4. _____

5. _____

6. _____

Mom,   clean
   My room is (clen.)

   I made it neet.

   May I go owt to play

   with the tem now?
                        Jan

Objectives: Children write missing spelling words to complete a question and a list of steps and proofread written work.

At-Home Activity: With your child, write a question using some of the spelling words. Include a question mark at the end of the question.

● Use ABC Order

Write the words in ABC order.   **eat give clean**

1. _____   2. _____   3. _____

▲ Test Yourself

Trace	Copy	Cover and Write
4. _eat_	_____	_____
5. _clean_	_____	_____
6. _neat_	_____	_____
7. _team_	_____	_____
8. _meat_	_____	_____
9. _give_	_____	_____

For Tomorrow

➡ See the word.

◇ Say it slowly.

▢ Link sounds and letters.

▽ Write.

⬠ Check.

Share What ea words did you find?

LESSON 33

Name ....

Words With ay

Spelling Words

day
may
say
stay
way
come (LOOKOUT WORD)

● **See and Say**

day   say
may   stay

▲ **Sounds and Letters**

-ay

1. _____   4. _____

2. _____   5. _____

3. _____   6. _____ (LOOKOUT WORD)

■ **Write and Check**

How do you tell your dog not to move?

7. You _____ " _____ ."

Objectives: Children recognize long *a* words with the *ay* pattern; spell the high-frequency word *come*; and write each spelling word.

At-Home Activity: With your child, search for words with *ay* on street or road signs, or for objects whose names rhyme with *day*.

● **Say and Write**
Read the riddle "Who Am I?"
Write the missing spelling words.

1. I _____ up all night.

2. You _____ find me in a nest.

3. I _____ "hoot, hoot."

▲ **Work With Opposites**
Write the spelling words that mean
the opposite.

4. night _____

5. go _____ _____

6. may not _____

Objectives: Children say and write the spelling words that complete
clues in a riddle and write spelling words that are antonyms.

At-Home Activity: With your child, create a two-line poem using
spelling words and other words that rhyme.

Words With *ay* 137

Word Hunt
Look on a calendar
for ay words.

SPELL CHAT

Can you think of
any other words that
rhyme with **day**?

Spelling Words	
day	stay
may	way
say	come

Name . . . .

Spelling Words

day
may
say
stay
way
come

Quick Write

Write about a place you like to go. Use three spelling words.

● **Write a Sentence**

Write the missing spelling words.

1. I _____ it is that _____ .

▲ **Proofread**

Jay found one word he spelled wrong.
Circle three more words spelled wrong.
Write the words on the lines.

2. _____

3. _____

4. _____

day
A ⟨da⟩ at May Park is fun.

I sta to see the animals.

They may com my way.

Then I gv them food.

Jay

Objectives: Children use spelling words to complete a sentence and proofread written work.

At-Home Activity: With your child, write a sentence, using a spelling word that tells what an animal might say.

Name ....

Use ABC Order

Write the words in ABC order. **stay come day**

1. _____   2. _____   3. _____

For Tomorrow

⇨ See the word.

◇ Say it slowly.

▢ Link sounds and letters.

▽ Write.

⬢ Check.

Test Yourself

Trace   Copy   Cover and Write

4. _day_ _____   _____   _____

5. _may_ _____   _____   _____

6. _say_ _____   _____   _____

7. _stay_ _____   _____   _____

8. _way_ _____   _____   _____

9. _come_ _____   _____   _____

Share What *ay* words did you find?

Objectives: Children write words in alphabetical order and self-test by tracing, copying, and then writing from memory each spelling word.

At-Home Activity: Help your child get ready for the spelling test by giving him or her a practice test.

Words With *ay* **139**

LESSON 34

Spelling Words

go

so

no

do

to

what

Learn and Spell   Name

Words With o

● **See and Say**

go
so

do
to

▲ **Sounds and Letters**

rhymes with

rhymes with

1. _____

2. _____

3. _____

4. _____

5. _____

6. _____ *LOOKOUT WORD*

■ **Write and Check**

What do you do if a tiger asks you to play?

7. You _____ _____ play.

Objectives: Children recognize the patterns when *o* follows a consonant; spell high-frequency word *what*; and write each spelling word.

At-Home Activity: Look in books or on signs for words that end with *o*. Help your child decide if the *o* sounds like the *o* in *go* or the *o* in *do*.

● Say and Write

Say each picture name.
What spelling word begins the same way?

1. _____

2. _____

3. _____

4. _____

5. _____

6.  _____

▲ Work With Words

Finish the story.
Write the missing spelling words.

7. _____ you want _____ play ball?

8. No. I must _____ home.

Objectives: Children write spelling words that have the same beginning sounds as picture names and write spelling words to complete sentences.

At-Home Activity: Write a note to your child. Help him or her use spelling words to answer the note.

Word Hunt
Look around your classroom and at home for words that end with o.

SPELL CHAT

Think of a sentence you can make with **go** and **do**.

Spelling Words	
go	do
so	to
no	what

Name ....

Spelling Words

go
so
no
do
to
what

Quick Write
Write about a time you stayed up late. Use three spelling words.

● **Write Words**

Use spelling words to finish the question and answer.

1. _____ you go _____ bed at ?

2. _____ . I _____ to bed at 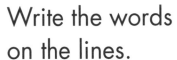 .

▲ **Proofread**

Noah found one word he spelled wrong. Circle three more words spelled wrong. Write the words on the lines.

do
"Why (doo) you look soe sad?"

3. _____ said Rob Rooster.

"I was late for the bus," said Pam Pig.

4. _____ "I lik to sleep."

5. _____ "Then you must go tu bed on time," said Rob.

Objectives: Children write words to complete sentences and proofread written work.

At-Home Activity: Discuss some rules your child thinks would be good to follow. Your child can write one rule, using some spelling words.

● Use ABC Order

Write the words in ABC order. **so   what   no**

1. _____ 2. _____ 3. _____

▲ Test Yourself

Trace	Copy	Cover and Write
4. go		
5. so		
6. no		
7. do		
8. to		
9. what		

For Tomorrow

⟹ See the word.

◇ Say it slowly.

☐ Link sounds and letters.

▽ Write.

⬡ Check.

Share What words did you find that end with o?

Objectives: Children write words in alphabetical order and self-test by tracing, copying, and then writing from memory each spelling word.

At-Home Activity: Help your child get ready for the spelling test by giving him or her a practice test.

LESSON 35

Name ....

Words With y

See and Say

b**y**   fl**y**
m**y**   tr**y**

Spelling Words

by
my
fly
try
why
been LOOKOUT WORD

▲ Sounds and Letters

-y

1. _____

2. _____

3. _____

4. _____

5. _____

6. _____ LOOKOUT WORD

■ Write and Check

I can do what my name says. What am I?

_____

7. a _____

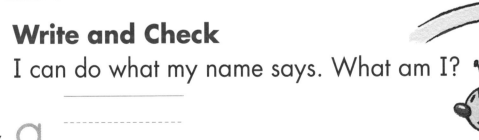

Objectives: Children recognize long *i* words with the *y* pattern; spell the high-frequency word *been;* and write each spelling word.

At-Home Activity: Together, play "I Spy" with words that end with *y* and rhyme with the word *I.* For example, *I spy the word* my.

Word Practice

Name ....

● Say and Write

Say the picture name. Write the spelling
word or words that begin the same way.

1. _____

3. _____

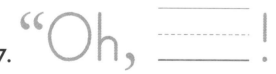
5. _____

2. _____

4. _____

6. _____

▲ Write With Rhymes

Write the missing spelling words.
Circle the words that rhyme with **I**.

7. "Oh, _____ !

8. _____ do I see a) in the sky ?

9. I will _____ to _____ ."

Word Hunt
Look in song books
for words that
rhyme with **I**.

SPELL CHAT

What two spelling words
are action words?

Spelling Words	
by	try
my	why
fly	been

Objectives: Children write spelling words that begin with the same
sounds as picture names and write spelling words to complete sentences.

At-Home Activity: With your child, write simple sentences that begin
with the words *I try to.* Then take turns acting out the sentences.

Name . . . .

Spelling Words

| by |
| my |
| fly |
| try |
| why |
| been |

Quick Write
Write about your birthday. Use two spelling words.

● **Write Words**
Write the missing spelling words.

_____ dad took me _____ bus.

We went to Lee Park.

Have you _____ there?

▲ **Proofread**
Maria found one word she spelled wrong.
Circle three more words spelled wrong.
Write the words on the lines.

1. _____

2. _____

3. _____

Dear Mom,
My
(Mi) plane will not fli.

I will tri to fix it.

Can you help mee?

Maria

Objectives: Children complete sentences using spelling words and proofread written work.

At-Home Activity: With your child, use spelling words to write to someone about a special place you both have been.

● Use ABC Order
Write these words in ABC order.   **been   fly   by**

1. _____   2. _____   3. _____

▲ Test Yourself

Trace	Copy	Cover and Write
4. by		
5. my		
6. fly		
7. try		
8. why		
9. been		

For Tomorrow

▭⟹ See the word.

◇ Say it slowly.

▢ Link sounds and letters.

▽ Write.

⬡ Check.

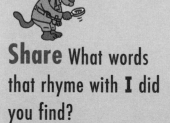

Share What words that rhyme with **I** did you find?

Objectives: Children write words in alphabetical order and self-test by tracing, copying, and then writing from memory each spelling word.

At-Home Activity: Help your child get ready for the spelling test by giving him or her a practice test.

Name...

Play Sammy Says

Help tell what Sammy says.
Write the missing spelling words.

out   eat

give   say

come   do

Sammy Says:

1. _____ not look.

2. _____ here.

3. Go _____ the ☐.

4. _____ a 🍌.

5. _____ me a hug.

6. _____ goodbye!

....

Objectives: Children write spelling words to complete directions.

At-Home Activity: Play "Sammy Says" with your child. Help your child write a new command that uses a spelling word.

● **Picture Rhymes**
Write spelling words that
rhyme with the picture names.

| see | go | neat |
| way | to | been |

1. _____

2. _____

3. _____

4. _____

5. _____

6. _____

▲ **Write the Secret Message**
The numbers match the words you wrote above.
Write the missing spelling words.

7. Here is a _____ _____
    (1)   (2)

_____ make funny faces.
(5)

Objectives: Children write spelling words that rhyme with names for pictures and create a coded message by matching numbers to spelling words they wrote.

At-Home Activity: Have your child say and write spelling words that rhyme with *you*, *play*, and/or *no*.

do my

why what

to

Story Time

Kangaroo wrote a story.
He left out some words.
Write the missing words.

Do you know _____
(1)

I like to _____? I like
(2)

_____ play ball. _____
(3)   (4)

team always wins.

Can you tell _____?
(5)

Objectives: Children write spelling words to finish a story.

At-Home Activity: With your child, write a sentence or two about something that is fun to do. Use some spelling words.

Name ....

Write the Right Word

Read each sentence.
Write the correct word.

meet   neat   been   eat   go

1. I have _____ good!   **Ben**
                             been

2. My room is _____.   **net**
                             neat

3. I _____ Papa.   **meet**
                             met

4. We _____ to the park.   **got**
                                go

5. We see the _____!   **at**
                             eat

Objectives: Children write spelling words to complete sentences.

At-Home Activity: Encourage your child to make a poster that uses one of the spelling words on the page.

Review 151

Spelling Matters!

Read Ted's poster for his door.

This is a net room.

My friend thought I had a **net** in my room. I really have a **neat** room!

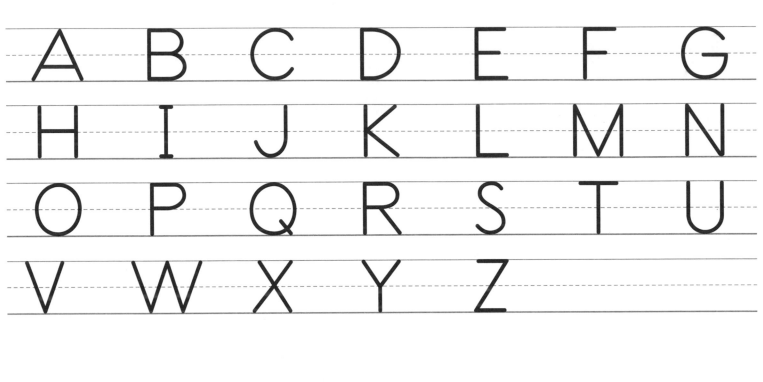

A B C D E F G
H I J K L M N
O P Q R S T U
V W X Y Z

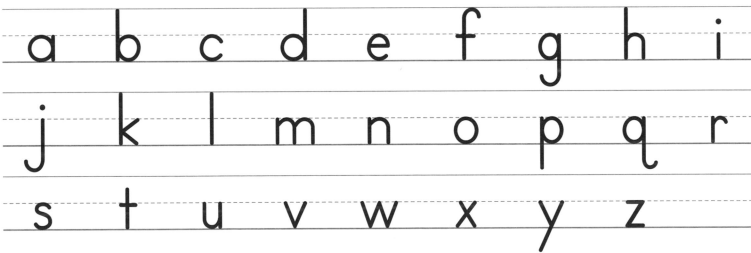

a b c d e f g h i
j k l m n o p q r
s t u v w x y z

and	get	make	the
are	give	may	they
ate	got	me	those
been	had	my	time
came	has	no	to
can	he	not	we
come	her	of	what
day	his	one	why
do	home	out	will
dog	hope	read	with
eat	I	say	you
for	is	see	
fun	like	she	

You will find all your spelling words in ABC order in the Spelling Dictionary. This page shows you how to use it.

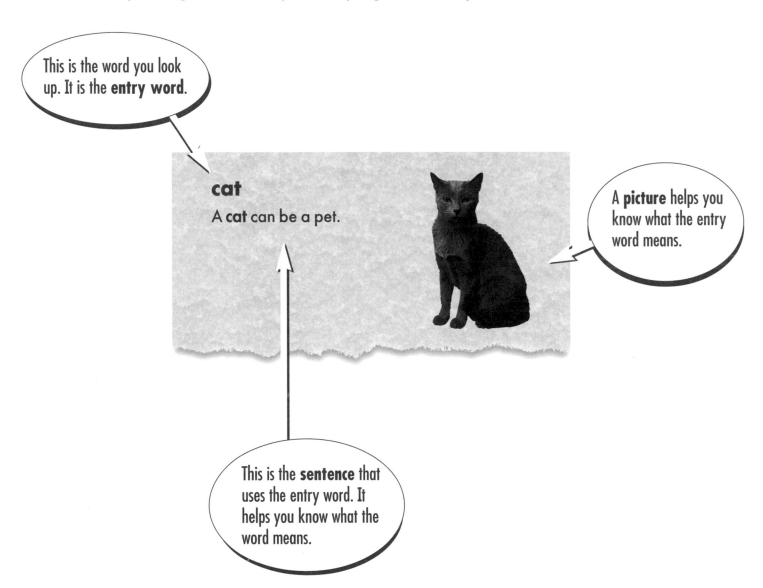

This is the word you look up. It is the **entry word**.

A **picture** helps you know what the entry word means.

cat
A **cat** can be a pet.

This is the **sentence** that uses the entry word. It helps you know what the word means.

Aa

agree
We **agree** on how to play the game.

and
The boy **and** the girl have a dog.

are
We **are** in art class.

ate
I **ate** my lunch.

Bb

bad
It is a **bad** day to go outside.

Spelling Dictionary

bag

What is in the **bag**?

be

What will you **be** when you grow up?

beast

A tiger is a **beast**.

bed

I made my **bed**.

bee

I saw a **bee** fly by.

been
The house has **been** sold.

beg
The dog can **beg**.

best
This is the **best** book!

big
An elephant is **big**.

birthday
Today is his **birthday**.

bubble
The **bubble** will pop.

bug
This **bug** is small.

but
A car is big, **but** a truck is bigger.

butterfly
A **butterfly** is an insect.

button
A **button** fell off my coat.

by

He is **by** the door.

Cc

came

He **came** to my house.

can

They **can** ride.

cat

A **cat** can be a pet.

clean

The dog will be **clean**.

come

The children **come** to school.

creep

Bugs **creep** along slowly.

cut

She can **cut** the paper.

Dd

day

What **day** is it?

did

Did you water the plants?

dig

The pig can **dig** a hole.

do

Do you want to swim?

dog
This is my **dog**.

Ee

eat
He likes to **eat** apples.

end
I like the **end** of the book.

Ff

fed
She **fed** the cat.

fill
He can **fill** the cup.

fit
The hat does not **fit**.

fly
Bats can **fly**.

fog
The **fog** is hiding the house.

for
This bag is **for** books.

frog
The **frog** can hop.

fun
It is **fun** to play tag.

funny
The book was **funny**.

Gg

get
Mom will **get**
the cat down.

give
He will **give** him the tape.

go
We will **go** when the light
is green.

got
He **got** a new shirt.

green
The plant is **green**.

Hh

had
The dogs **had** fun.

has
She **has** a kitten.

hat
A **hat** is for your head.

he

He likes to read.

help

I **help** my brother.

hen

This **hen** is brown.

her

Her coat is wet.

hid

The cat **hid** the hat.

hide

We can **hide** in the tree.

hill

The trees are on the **hill**.

his

His tire is flat.

hit

You can **hit** the ball with the bat.

hog

A **hog** is a grown pig.

home
We are going **home**.

hop
This animal can **hop**.

hope
I **hope** you feel better.

hot
The stove is **hot**.

hug
I like to **hug** my mom.

Ii

I
I like my shoes.

is

She **is** my mom.

Ll

late

He is **late** for school.

leg

The girl hurt her **leg**.

let

Mom **let** us play longer.

letter

He is writing a **letter** to Grandma.

like
I **like** bananas.

log
This **log** was cut from a tree.

Mm

make
We will **make** a cake.

may
May I have milk, please?

me
Can you see **me**?

meat

I like to eat **meat**.

meet

It is nice to **meet** you.

mine

This coat is **mine**.

my

This is **my** school.

Nn

neat

The room is **neat**.

no
No, thank you.

nose
I smell with my **nose**.

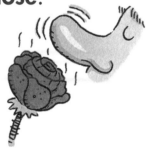

not
Do **not** put trash on the ground.

Oo

of
The pig made a house **of** sticks.

one
The number **one** comes before two.

1 2 3

out
Dad took **out** the milk.

Pp

pancakes
I like **pancakes**!

pet
This is my **pet** dog.

pig
This **pig** has spots.

pillow
The **pillow** is soft.

pin
I put a **pin** in my picture.

planet
Mars is a **planet**.

play
I **play** with my friends.

popcorn
I like to eat **popcorn**.

Rr

ran
They **ran** fast.

read

I like to **read** my book.

red

An apple is **red**.

riddle

I can tell you a **riddle**.

ride

I like to **ride** my bike.

rode

She **rode** a horse.

rub

We **rub** the cars.

rug

The **rug** is blue.

run

The rabbit likes to **run**.

Ss

sad

He is **sad**.

sat

She **sat** down.

say
He can **say** my name.

Kim!

scream
I **scream** when my team wins.

see
Can you **see** the whale?

she
She is my grandma.

shine
I like my shoes to **shine**.

shut
Please **shut** the door on your way out.

shy
He becomes **shy** when he meets someone new.

silly
This is a **silly** game.

sit
We **sit** on the rug to read.

sleep
They **sleep** in their beds.

smile

I **smile** when I am happy.

snake

The **snake** is long.

so

I was sick, **so** I went to bed.

soft

The sheep is **soft**.

spill

A drink can **spill**.

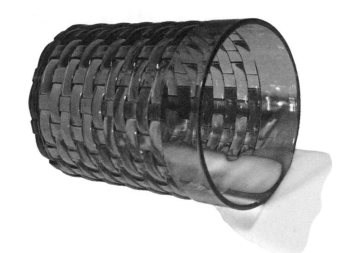

spin

It is fun to **spin** the top.

stay

My puppy must **stay** home when I go to school.

still

We had to stand **still** for our picture.

stone

I like this **stone** the best.

sun

The **sun** is hot.

Tt

take
You should **take** your coat.

team
We play on a **team**.

telephone
Call me on the **telephone**.

ten
We have **ten** toes.

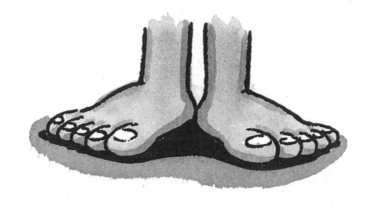

the
The car stops.

they
They are my friends.

those
I want **those**!

three
One and two make **three**.

time
It is **time** to eat.

to
I like to go **to** the beach.

too

I have a cat.
I have a dog, **too**.

top

I am on **top**!

tree

The **tree** is tall.

try

The baby will **try** to walk.

tub

This **tub** is pink.

Ww

wag

Dogs **wag** their tails.

wagon
The horses pull
the **wagon**.

way
This is the **way**
to my room.

we
We ride the bus.

what
What is for lunch?

who
Who wants to go
outside?

why
Why is the sky blue?

wiggle
Worms **wiggle**.

will
We **will** swim.

win
He will **win** the race.

with
I play ball **with** Dad.

Yy

you
You can play, too.

A a

B b

C c

D d

E e

F f

G g

H h

I i

J j

K k

L l

M m

N n

O o

P p

Q q

R r

S s

T t

U u

V v

W w

X x

Y y

Z z